A
Simple
Gita

by
Vraja Kishor

First Edition: *Mohiṇī Ekādaśī* - May 21, 2013

ISBN: 148952522X
ISBN-13: 978-1489525222

CONTENTS

INTRODUCTION

By now there are certainly many, many English editions of *Bhagavad-Gītā*, but so far as I know, none of them is at all like this one: a simple, enjoyable dialogue flowing naturally, allowed to explain itself at its own pace.

Bhagavad-Gītā is a relatively small (yet undeniably essential) section of the epic drama, *Mahābhārata*. Many complex characters and plots from that story make a brief appearance in the *Gītā's* first chapter. I intentionally ignore as many as possible, trying to keep the focus on the *Gītā* itself, not *Mahābhārata*.

I owe a great debt to A.C. Bhaktivedānta Swāmī Prabhupāda for introducing me to the *Gītā* and creating the gurus (especially Śrīla Dhanurdhara Swāmī) who very kindly and personally taught it to me. If you want to study this dialogue in more detail, referencing the original Sanskrit, you would find his <u>Bhagavad-Gītā As It Is</u> an exceptional resource.

I am similarly indebted to Śrīla Viśvanātha Cakravartī. His astounding presentation of *Gītā,* entitled <u>Sārārtha-varṣiṇī-ṭīkā</u>, utilized Arjuna's voice as a compelling medium for delivering commentary. I have tried to follow his lead, voicing Arjuna's implicit questions, and occasionally making brief clarifying statements through him.

I am also grateful to my wife, not only for being an outstanding example of so many principles in the Gītā, but especially for painting the cover illustration for this book. And I am in the debt of Kadamba Māla dāsī for volunteering her excellent skills as a proofreader, and to Balajhi Devanathan for his contribution towards printing.

The *Gītā* enjoys its tremendous fame and cultural importance because it clearly and succinctly brings out the unity in so many apparently diverse strands of Indian philosophy and spiritual culture. I hope my presentation of this treasure will be a book you can both leisurely enjoy and carefully contemplate.

May the message of Śrī Krishna's all-attractive words illuminate your heart, as the full autumn moon illuminates the dazzling white lotus of divine love.

~ 1 ~

INESCAPABLE DEPRESSION

1[i]

A blind, old king asked:

What happened when my sons gathered for war against my brother's sons, on the sacred field of Kurukṣetra?

2-13

His minister answered:

Your eldest son studied the opposing army and went to speak to his teacher. "Gurudeva," he said. "Look at the formidable army that opposes us. It is full of warriors as mighty as Arjuna, all under the expert

---

[i] These numbers reference the original Sanskrit texts.

command of your own disciple. Yet, compare them to my army. I have you and so many other ever-victorious warriors, like Grandfather Bhīṣma; each one well-armed, experienced, and ready to die for my sake. The opponent is powerful, but with Bhīṣma on my side, my power is limitless."

Turning to his troops he announced, "All of you rally around the great Bhīṣma!"

Bhīṣma then blew his conch, signaling all the other trumpets, bugles and drums to resound deafeningly - delighting the King's son.

14-27

The opposing army responded immediately and fearlessly - blowing their remarkable divine conch shells to create a deafening sound that crushed the hearts of their opponents.

The great hero Arjuna took up his bow to begin the fight, but suddenly he hesitated and said to Krishna, "Drive our chariot midway out... so I can better see those who have sided with evil."

Krishna did, and said, with a hint of sarcasm and foreshadowing, "Here, my friend, have a look at your entire family."

Scattered among the two armies, Arjuna saw fathers, grandfathers, teachers, uncles, brothers, sons, grandsons, friends, in-laws and well-wishers. He was deeply shaken.

28-30

Arjuna: My dear Krishna, when I see all of these relatives prepared to kill one another, my spirit recoils. Shivering with goose-bumps and pinpricks, I can't seem to keep my bow in my hands. I am being overwhelmed by the urge to run as far away as possible, before I go mad! Everywhere I look, all I can see is horrific misery about to devour us.

31-35

Krishna: You have done *everything possible* to avoid this war: your whole family lived in the forest for a dozen years, you all spent another year in servitude and hiding, all while tolerating a string of ruthless assassination attempts. No matter what you do, your enemy forever refuses to compromise. What option remains but war? There is no other way to regain what was wrongly taken from your family.

Arjuna: No, this will backfire! Nothing good can come from killing my family. And even if something good *did* come from it, how would I enjoy it with their blood on my hands? And even if I could enjoy it, *who* would I enjoy it with?

Even to gain the entire universe, one shouldn't kill one's own relatives!

36

Krishna: *Relatives?* You still want to call these people "relatives"? They tried again and again to kill you and your whole family. They are not relatives, they are

~ 2 ~

SPIRITUAL KNOWLEDGE

11

Krishna: You use words that wise men use, but do you really comprehend them? I doubt it, because you are crippled by your emotions, and that never happens to the truly wise. Nothing in life or death causes the wise to breakdown as you have.

12

Arjuna: Why are the wise not shaken by death?

Krishna: Because we never really die. I have always existed. You have always existed. All these people around you have always existed…and we always will exist.

13

Arjuna: Then, what is death?

Krishna: It is a change of form.

Life-force constantly changes form. Even in this one lifetime it transforms from childhood into youth and eventually to old-age. At the end of this lifetime it transforms into an entirely new form. Wise people are not confused about this.[i]

14-15

Arjuna: Nonetheless, the death of loved ones is a very unpleasant "transformation."

Krishna: Of course! But *pleasant* and *unpleasant* are merely sensations - superficial side effects of our external senses gaining or losing contact with external things. Like summer and winter, pleasure and displeasure come and go on their own.

Arjuna: Well, "superficial" things also have their significance.

Krishna: Yes, but don't make important decisions based on them! If sensations interfere with your important duties, just *tolerate* them and do not falter in your duty. This attitude will liberate you from *karma*.

---

[i] *The law of conservation of energy - "energy is never lost, it merely changes form" - also applies to life-energy. It has always existed and will always exist – although it constantly changes form.*

16

Arjuna: How can I become deep and wise enough to do that?

Krishna: Learn to see the difference between real and unreal, permanent and temporary, life-force and its external form.

Arjuna: Please explain this in detail! What is the difference between the real and unreal?

Krishna: If something can be destroyed, it does not truly exist. If something truly exists, it cannot be destroyed. People who can see this have real vision.

17

Arjuna: What is the indestructible thing that really exists?

Krishna: The indestructible reality is the thing that is everywhere, pervading everything.

Arjuna: What is that?

Krishna: Life-force, the soul.

18-19

Arjuna: What is the unreal thing, sure to be destroyed?

Krishna: The body - the temporary, external form of the indestructible and infinite soul.

Now, imagine a wise person in your position - faced with the extremely unpleasant duty of fighting a war against his own family. What would he do?

Arjuna: I don't know.

Krishna: He would fight!

Arjuna: How would he be able to cope with the debilitating emotional pain and confusion?

Krishna: With the meditation, "I cannot be killed, nor can I kill anyone else. We are all a spiritual substance that cannot kill or be killed."

20-21

Arjuna: Why should I believe that the soul is not destroyed or damaged when its body dies?

Krishna: You must have heard this statement from the Upanishad:[i] "Never created, never destroyed; without past, present or future; it is unborn, eternal, ever-existing, and primeval. It is not killed when the body dies."

My friend, a civilized person like you must have considered these statements before. You must know that the soul is indestructible and eternal, unborn, and undying. So why do you fear that you will hurt or kill anyone?

22

Arjuna: What happens to the soul when its body dies?

Krishna: When the soul releases one body it takes

---

[i] Viz. Kaṭha Upaniṣad (1.2.18)

another - just like you get new clothes to replace old ones that have worn out.

23-24

Arjuna: How can the soul not be damaged or destroyed by such a catastrophic change?

Krishna: Life-force is simply *impervious*. You can't cut it with a blade; you can't burn it with flame; you can't dissolve it in water; nor erode it with the wind.

Unbreakable, unburnable, insoluble, un-erodible life-force pervades everything and is everlasting, immovable, and eternally independent.

25

Arjuna: Why is the soul impervious?

Krishna: Those who have realized what life-force is describe it as non-manifest and beyond-conception - it is not really even "in" its body. It is beyond. That's why it is impervious to anything affecting its body.

Therefore death should not cause you to lament so deeply that you abandon your duties.

26

Arjuna: Your whole argument rests on the idea that life cannot be destroyed; and you back up this idea by referring to the statements of scriptures and "realized sages." What if I don't really trust those statements?

Krishna: Alright, my brave friend, let's accept the position that life itself is created at birth and destroyed at death. Still, death should not shake you so deeply.

27-28

Arjuna: Why not?

Krishna: Let's say that at birth we emerge from nothingness, and at death we merge back into nothingness. If this is so, then what is death but a return to the original state from which we were born? When we return to that state, surely the same sequence of events that brought us into being once will eventually bring us into being again.

You might accept the statements of sages, or you might speculate with logic, but from either angle death is sure to follow birth, and birth is sure to follow death.

29

Arjuna: Indeed some philosophers express this point of view. Why?

Krishna: There are many different opinions on this subject because anything concerning the soul will naturally be difficult to understand, either by direct perception, logic, or inquiry.

30

Arjuna: Which version is closer to the truth: an eternally distinct soul that is indestructible and survives death, or rebirth in the vague sense of fluctuating in and out of nothingness?

Krishna: Life-force, which animates all things, is distinctly eternal and indestructible. That is my opinion, my friend.

So, you should not allow the natural grief of death to grip you so hard that you flee from your responsibilities. Under no circumstances should you hesitate to suffer any trial in the effort to fulfill your responsibilities.

31-33

Arjuna: Please clarify what my responsibilities are. I have become so disoriented.

Krishna: You are a warrior. Your greatest responsibility is to fight to protect a good cause. Warriors who fight for such causes, without selfish motive, find the gates of paradise open wide.

If you don't take up your role in this fight, you will neglect your responsibilities. Thus you will lose your glory and gain the stain of guilt.

34

Arjuna: At this point, I really don't mind.

Krishna: Oh please. You are a moral person. For someone like you dishonor is worse than death! You know that. And if you flee this battle, people will proclaim your dishonor forever!

35-36

Arjuna: Maybe they will honor me as a good man

who renounced the world for the sake of non-violence.

Krishna: Arjuna, we are talking about *warriors!* They hold you in the highest esteem now, but if you flee the battle they will only be able to think that you fled out of cowardice!

They will terribly slander and condemn you. What could be more painful?

37

Arjuna: This battle is more painful!

Krishna: No, the battle will not lead to pain. If you win you will enjoy a great kingdom. If you lose you will enjoy paradise. So *stand up,* Arjuna! Fight without doubts!

38

Arjuna: I disagree. The pain of this battle outweighs the pleasure of a kingdom or paradise.

Krishna: Then you must elevate your mind and act from a less selfish platform. We must do whatever is our duty. Ignore pleasure and displeasure, loss and gain, victory and defeat... treat them all the same and fight merely because it is your duty to do so. Then you will never incur *karma.*

39

Arjuna: To elevate my mind requires great intelligence. Where can I get such intelligence?

Krishna: People usually describe "intelligence" as something scholastic, but I will explain it in a practical way. *Practical intelligence* will elevate and liberate you from the bonds of action and reaction.

40

Arjuna: Can someone like me hope to realize such intelligence?

Krishna: Even if you do not fully comprehend, any progress you make towards it is a great gain, a treasure that will dispel your fears and will never fade or disappear!

41

Arjuna: How should I strive towards it?

Krishna: Strive for it with resolute focus. Do not let your ambitions scatter away from it, towards countless distractions.

42-45

Arjuna: What are the distractions to beware of?

Krishna: The scattered thoughts of fools rush towards the flowery promises of materialistic culture, thinking, "This is all there is!" Their hearts are set on pleasure and paradise, in hopes of name and fame; and they make so many elaborate efforts towards power and enjoyment.

Those whose hearts are stolen by addiction to power and enjoyment can never have resolute focus, *samādhi*.

Materialistic culture, even if it is "Vedic," focuses on sense objects produced by the three qualities of illusion. Rise above this, Arjuna! The promises of material happiness are a dense and dark forest that you must find the way out of. Become singularly resolute, grounded in what is everlastingly real, and unconcerned with acquisition. Then you will tangibly grasp your own self!

46

Arjuna: But materialistic culture, especially the Vedic variety, serves a purpose. It *gradually* reforms materialistic people. Isn't it dangerous or wrong to completely reject it?

Krishna: Whatever you can get from a small well you can certainly get from a deep lake! Whatever true benefit comes from materialistic culture is easily attained by one who deeply realizes spirit.

47-49

Arjuna: Alright, I accept that I should focus exclusively on spiritual knowledge. How do I begin?

Krishna: First, understand that you can't control whether your actions will succeed or fail. All you can control is whether or not you will try. So concentrate on fulfilling your responsibilities without yearning for a pleasant result, or fleeing from an unpleasant one.

When you have equanimity towards the success or failure of your actions, then your deeds become *yoga* - an expression of wisdom and intelligence. Try to come under the shelter of this wise attitude towards work. Avoid giving up your duties when they are unpleasant, like an irresponsible and selfish fool chasing pleasure haphazardly.

50

Arjuna: If I act without striving for a result, what will result from such actions?

Krishna: Liberation! Such selfless *"karmas"* liberate you from good and bad *karma* alike. So strive for this *yoga* - the "art of action."

51

Arjuna: How can *karma* grant liberation from *karma*?

Krishna: When you don't strive for the results of your endeavors, you are released from the bondage to those results. You become a great soul, liberated from birth and death, and situated in a condition free from infirmity.

52-53

Arjuna: But my emotions break free from my weak resolve and pull me always towards selfish interests.

Krishna: You must make the effort to reclaim your intellect from the brambles of delusion! Work hard to make your intellect steady, undisturbed, immovable, and unwavering in the *samādhi* of *yoga*. Then no promises of materialistic culture will attract or disgust you.

54

Arjuna: Please tell me about the qualities of such *yogis*, deep people with practical intelligence who have attained *samādhi*. What do they talk about? How do they sit still? How do they walk around?

55

Krishna: If you attain practical intelligence, your main quality will be total disinterest in the fleeting desires that roam your mind.

Arjuna: Why?

Krishna: Because all your deepest desires will already be satisfied from within your own soul. Therefore you won't be aggravated by pleasures and displeasures that flicker shallowly through your emotions. You will be sagaciously dispassionate, fearless, and tranquil.

56

Arjuna: Now please explain how the active yogi moves about?

Krishna: If you attain practical intelligence, your movements will neither be towards nor away from any external object. You will make no effort to gain or lose anything, because you will have no special affection for anything in this external world.

57

Arjuna: Please answer how the active yogi talks.

Krishna: Become deeply fixed in practical intelligence, and you will never particularly praise or criticize any success or failure.

58

Arjuna: Please also answer the last question about how an active yogi sits still.

Krishna: Realize practical intelligence and you will withdraw absolutely from *selfish* action. Your senses will pull away from the exploitation of sense objects like a turtle withdrawing into its shell.

59-60

Arjuna: How is it *possible* to detach the senses from their desired objects!?

Krishna: It is impossible if you try to do it by force, struggling to repress enjoyment while still hungry for it. Even the most resolute and determined cannot fully succeed in that endeavor. But it *is* possible to detach from sensual enjoyment as a natural side-effect of enjoying something else, something *better*.

61

Arjuna: How can we experience a pleasure that will make us disinterested in selfish sensual exploits?

Krishna: Experience *me!* Fix your senses and your actions on me, on *my* pleasure. Then your senses will happily and easily come under your control.

62-63

Arjuna: Is there any other way to 'sit still' and control the senses?

Krishna: No.

Arjuna: Why not?

Krishna: As soon as your senses experience any object, you form an opinion of it. From this opinion comes the desire to acquire or avoid the object. This desire inevitably leads, eventually, to anger and frustration - for desire is impossible to completely satisfy. Anger and frustration always lead quickly to confusion. Confusion causes us to forget our principles, to make unintelligent choices, and brings about our own ruination.

64-65

Arjuna: But practical intelligence also involves interaction between the senses and their objects. Does this disastrous sequence of events affect the practical yogi, too?

Krishna: No.

Arjuna: Why not?

Krishna: Because they act out of *devotion*. The sincere effort to regulate your attractions and repulsions by fixing your senses on me is a devotional act, which invokes *divine compassion*.

That divine compassion quickly destroys sorrow and distress, and makes your happy heart still and steady in practical intelligence. It protects you from that disastrous sequence.

Arjuna: What *is* this "divine compassion"?

Krishna: It is the constitutional *joy* that naturally results by experiencing me.

66

Arjuna: Without the inner joy of divine compassion, no one can hope to control their senses intelligently?

Krishna: It's impossible. Without divine compassion your intelligence cannot control your senses. And if the intelligence cannot control the senses, your heart will not experience itself. If your heart cannot experience itself, you will not experience peace. If you cannot experience peace, you will never be happy.

67-68

Arjuna: But intelligence is *superior* to the senses. Why should the senses be able escape its control and even become its master?

Krishna: The senses accomplish this by distracting the intellect, just like the wind can push a sailboat off course. Even a mighty warrior like you can be dragged around by your senses! It takes very firm intelligence to restrain the senses from their natural objectives.

69

Arjuna: What is it like to have control of the senses?

Krishna: When your intellect takes command of your senses, you will yawn at things that so titillate the common man; and be aroused by things they yawn at.

70-72

Arjuna: How do I begin the quest to control my senses?

Krishna: Don't be like the sailboat, be like the ocean. The ocean is always being filled by the incessant flow of rivers, but it remains steady and does not rise. You should similarly *tolerate* the incessant flow of sensual desires. This will gradually calm the energy of desire that fuels the unruliness in your senses.

If you try to satisfy the flow of desires, you will never know peace. But if you tolerate that incessant river you become free from longing, possessiveness, and egoism; peace comes within reach.

My cousin, when you attain the spiritual peace that becomes available after intelligently controlling your senses, you will never again be confused! And when you can maintain this state even up till your end, you will gain the supreme spiritual peace *(nirvāṇa)*.

~ 3 ~

PRACTICAL PHILOSOPHY

1-2

Arjuna: You say that intelligence is more important than action, but then you push me into terrible actions? This is a confusing contradiction, so please tell me plainly - What is better for me, action or philosophy?

3

Krishna: I did not say intelligence is more important than action. I said you must *synthesize* the two paths: the science of philosophy and the practicality of action.

4

Arjuna: Why synthesize them? If philosophy is more

sublime, why shouldn't I dedicate myself to it completely?

Krishna: To completely dedicate yourself to philosophy you must put it into practice! True philosophy is not inactive, it is practical! No one becomes truly wise or free from worldliness by just sitting around doing nothing.

5

Arjuna: Why not?

Krishna: Because it is impossible to really do nothing. No one can pass a single moment without doing *something*. Everyone is helplessly forced to act, by their very nature.

6

Arjuna: What about those who live in the forest or in caves, doing nothing but meditation?

Krishna: Everyone knows they are pretenders! They keep their senses repressed, but their minds reminisce on sense objects.

7

Arjuna: How can one avoid being a pretender?

Krishna: Real sense-control can begin when you free your mind from selfishness by *using* your senses intelligently. That is far better than making a show of "giving up the world."

8

Arjuna: But how can I use the senses intelligently unless I first cultivate intelligence?

Krishna: At first you can *borrow* intelligence from the scriptures, by doing your duties responsibly. That is intelligent action. It is certainly better than trying to stop all activities. If you give up your activities you won't even be able to keep your body functioning properly!

9

Arjuna: But sensual action is supposed to be the cause of bondage!?

Krishna: Yes. Do *not* do anything for the sake of sensuality! Work only for the sake of sacrifice![i] If you work for your own worldly desires you will suffer degradation and bondage; but if you work as a sacrifice you will become perfectly liberated.

10-15

Arjuna: But even if I work selflessly, as a sacrifice, results will inevitably come to me, and I will inevitably enjoy them to some extent.

---

[i] There is a double-meaning here because the word 'Sacrifice' [Yajña] is widely used in Sanskrit as a proper name for Viṣṇu, the Supreme Personality of Godhead. Thus Krishna is saying two things at once: that we should work without selfish motive, and that we should work with the motive to please Godhead.

Krishna: That is fine. The side effects of duty are wholesome. When the Creator[i] created duties, he told the people:

May these duties make you prosperous and fulfill your every desire!

Please the gods by these duties, and the gods will bless you with everything you desire. Thus both of you will prosper. But if you try to prosper and enjoy without sacrifice, you become a thief subject to punishment!

That is why those who eat the food that remains after they feed others never suffer; while those who cook only for themselves eat their own demise.

Your bodies are made from the nutrients in food. Food comes from rain. Rain comes from nature. Do not try to steal from nature! The personified forces of nature are pleased when you are selfless and dutiful. Duties are defined by the Vedas, which are spiritual sound waves. Therefore duties are essentially spiritual. Follow these duties and you will prosper materially and spiritually.

16

Arjuna: In other words, it is righteous to be happy and healthy as a natural side effect of doing my duty?

---

[i] Here, Krishna paraphrases a statement of Brahmā, the origin of which is unknown to us.

Krishna: Yes, but trying to be "happy and healthy" without following this approach to life is *filthy*. Selfish people living like that are meaninglessly intoxicated by sensual pleasures.

17-19

Arjuna: Then should I do my duty for the sake of the side-effect I personally desire?

Krishna: That's not terrible, but I think you can do much better.

Arjuna: Please explain.

Krishna: Try to be satisfied by your own being; quench your thirsts from the well of your own soul; delight within yourself. Then you will have no personal need for action. You will be self-sustained and will have no ulterior motive for doing, or not doing, anything.

Strive for this way of life - fulfilling your responsibilities without ulterior motive. To work without personal attachment is the best catalyst of spiritual evolution.

20-24

Arjuna: Why would a purified and self-satisfied person take the trouble of doing any deeds, even moral and responsible ones?

Krishna: For the sake of others.

Whatever great people do, common people imitate. Whatever examples they set, the world adopts. Knowing this, many kings, like Janaka, attained perfection through the yoga of duty. You should do the same and set the right example for all your citizens and admirers.

You can also look at me as an example. I have no motive: no emptiness to fill, no goal unattained, no debt to repay to anyone in the three worlds. Yet still I responsibly perform all my duties with great care. Why? Because if I didn't, all of humanity would follow suit! Civilization would fall apart, replaced by calamity and confusion.[i]

25

Arjuna: So the wise and the fools *both* engage in worldly deeds?

Krishna: Yes, but with different motivations. Ignorant people work hard because they are driven by selfish motives. Wise people also work hard, but for the well-being of the world.

26

Arjuna: Why don't the wise just teach philosophy to the foolish?

---

[i] This addresses Arjuna's earlier argument that fighting would destroy civilization. Krishna presents the opposite argument: *not* fighting would set an example that would destroy civilization.

Krishna: How will a fool understand philosophy? The wise know better than to confuse them with impractical theories and concepts. Instead they set an example that encourages people to pursue their precious desires in a more moral, dutiful, and spiritually progressive way.

27

Arjuna: What is the key difference between the worldly deeds of a fool and the worldly deeds of the wise?

Krishna: The fool thinks with *ahaṁkāra* - "I am doing this. It is my action, and thus the result should also be mine to enjoy." But the truth is that everything he does is simply a part of a complex chain of cause and effect.

Wise people, on the other hand, understand the relationship between causality and action. Thus, unlike fools, they do not become personally wrapped up in their actions.

The knowledge of selfish fools is quite incomplete, and they have very little interest in changing that. Knowing this, the wise do not unnecessarily upset them with philosophy.

30

Arjuna: If I am a fool, how can I become wise?

Krishna: You must make a serious effort: Be spiritually aware and renounce all implication in activity by doing your duty only for *my* sake. Have no personal ambition in your deeds, no sense of entitlement to the results. Throw off your feebleness and do your duty in this state of mind. Fight!

31

Arjuna: But how can I not be afraid of the terrible destiny that will result from such brutal duties as lie before me?

Krishna: I already explained that destiny does not accrue to a person who does not act with the motive to enjoy destiny. You just need to comprehend and fully embrace what I have already said.

32

Arjuna: What if I cannot?

Krishna: Those who loathe and reject my advice become perfect fools in every way; ruined and thoughtless.

33

Arjuna: If I abandon my horrible duty to cultivate knowledge and philosophy I will be "ruined"? Why?

Krishna: No matter how philosophical or knowledgeable you try to become, you will always be *forced* to act. Your habitual nature *cannot* be repressed! You literally *cannot* give up the scenarios that surround your duty.

34

Arjuna: If it is impossible to stop sensual activities, how can I ever become spiritual?

Krishna: You can't repress, but you can *regulate* yourself. Become spiritual by regulating the attachment and repulsion between your senses and various objects. Control your senses; don't be controlled by them, for that would block the progressive path.

35

Arjuna: Fine, but let me regulate myself according to the codes of saints who dwell in the forest. Let me cast aside the codes of a warrior.

Krishna: That is not "regulation" - it is whimsy! Stick to *your own* duties, even if sometimes they are very difficult, or seem full of flaws. Don't jump onto someone else's path, even if it seems so much easier and better than yours. It is better to endure the difficulties of your own path, because to walk a path meant for another is very dangerous.

36

Arjuna: I cannot argue with this. Medicine is good, but to take medicine prescribed for someone else could be fatal. Yet still, I cannot stand up and face my responsibilities... What forces me away from wise deeds, even against my will?

37-39

Krishna: Selfishness. Selfish desires, which are born from passion and end in wrath.

Selfishness is all-consuming. It is the worst evil, your worst enemy. It eclipses your true self ever more thickly: like smoke covering a fire, dust covering a mirror, or even the womb covering a child. It devours wisdom like an insatiable inferno. It is the constant enemy of the wise.

40

Arjuna: Where does this powerful enemy encamp?

Krishna: Selfishness builds fortresses in your senses, emotions, and deep within your thoughts. From these bases it conquers you by bewildering the soul and eclipsing its wisdom.

41-42

Arjuna: How can I attack this enemy? What is his weak point?

Krishna: Attack selfishness by regulating the practical activities of your senses. Only then can you begin to defeat this villain who devours knowledge and wisdom.

Gradually progress from your senses to your emotions, and from your emotions to your thoughts. You can conquer and reclaim all these strategic locations because you, the soul, are superior to all of them.

43

Arjuna: Where can I draw strength for this battle?

Krishna: Become strong by centering yourself within your self, knowing that the real you is beyond and more powerful than even your thoughts. Then you can be victorious in the very difficult battle against your true enemy: selfishness.

~ 4 ~

THE PATH TO WISDOM

1-2

Arjuna: It seems that wisdom, intelligence, and philosophy are *key*. With them I can become spiritually centered and free from attachment to pleasure and displeasure, happiness and distress, success and failure.

What is the path to wisdom?

Krishna: Ultimately, wisdom comes from me. For example, I have been teaching you the yoga of practical philosophy; but what I am teaching is not new. It is contained in sacred texts and is embedded in our culture, because many saintly kings have already learned this subject. Ultimately, they learned it from the ancient king, Ikṣvāku, who learned it from his father Manu, who learned it from Vivasvān, the sun-god, who learned it from me.

As wisdom passes from one teacher to the next, it gradually becomes distorted, diluted, and eventually forgotten. Therefore I, the original teacher, have to periodically reintroduce the original science. Today I will do just that, by teaching it to you.

3

Arjuna: To me!? Why *me?*

Krishna: I have chosen you because I trust you, and you trust me.

Arjuna: Am I qualified to understand what you are teaching?

Krishna: You are devoted to me; you are my friend. Therefore you can certainly comprehend the ultimate secrets I will explain.

4

Arjuna: Then please explain how you could have taught anything to the sun-god, who was born a very long time before you.

5

Krishna: I have passed through many births. So have you. The difference is that I am aware of all of them, but you are not.

6

Arjuna: Why do you remember, while I forget?

Krishna: You forget because you invest your consciousness into an external body, which is always in the process of disappearing. Thus your memories fade. I am not the same as you. I only *seem* to have a body. The truth is that I am never born and never age. I am the proprietor and master of everything. My "body" is my own manifestation of the power within my own self.

7-8

Arjuna: Why do you take the trouble of manifesting yourself within this world?

Krishna: I must manifest myself whenever the paths of morality and wisdom are overgrown by weeds of immorality and confusion.

Arjuna: To repave the moral paths?

Krishna: Yes.

Arjuna: How?

Krishna: By protecting those who still walk upon them and destroying those who do not.

9-10

Arjuna: Do people avail themselves of the wisdom and morality you establish? And if so, what happens to them?

Krishna: Yes, those who understand that I am not an ordinary person avail themselves of my teachings. If you understand that my birth and my deeds are spiritual, you will avail yourself what I offer. Thus you will not take another birth when you leave your body. You will come to me.

Arjuna: That's possible?

Krishna: Yes. Many people have already done so. When their hearts became enraptured by knowing me, they could easily tolerate selfish desires, and the resulting fears and angers. Thus they became liberated, and attained me.

11

Arjuna: What about someone who tries to tolerate selfish desires but without any specific interest in you personally?

Krishna: Everyone walks on my path, and I give each one the reward that they come to me for.

12

Arjuna: What about people who seem to walk a path that doesn't include you at all?

Krishna: Such as?

Arjuna: Such as the materialists who worship so many gods.

Krishna: I created the path they walk. And I empower it to be effective. Desiring material success they make various sacrifices, and it is *I* who reciprocate by empowering the gods to quickly grant the petty things they desire.

13

Arjuna: What about those whose efforts don't even include the gods? Those who simply work at their careers, are they also on your path?

Krishna: Certainly. I create and empower human social systems as well. For example the four careers, distinguished from one another on the basis of practical qualifications, spring from me.[i]

Arjuna: So, indirectly they are all interacting with you, even though they are unaware of it?

Krishna: Yes.

---

[i] The "four careers" are four social roles based on four personality types: (1) Rare people are philosophical and intellectual. They function as the thinkers and guides of society - *"brāhmaṇa."* (2) Some people are unusually powerful. They function under the intellectuals as rulers, leaders, and enforcers - *"kṣatriya."* (3) Often, people are very resourceful and entrepreneurial. They function in business to generate wealth and social resources - *"vaiśya."* (4) Most people are simply obsessed with making ends meet with the meager skills they possess. They function as employees - *"śūdra."*

These terms may ring an unfriendly bell, sounding a lot like the deplorable, debilitating "caste system." The clear and all-important difference between the original system and its ruined pre-modern farce, however, is that one's position in the original is based on practical qualifications *("guṇa-karma-vibhāgaśa")* while in the modern farce it is based *solely* on birth *("janma-vibhāgaśa")*.

Arjuna: Well, why shouldn't I give up my social duties as a warrior and take the higher path of directly meditating on you?

Krishna: The social system is not only for materialists. I myself work within the social system, even though I am the transcendental non-doer. I already explained this.

14-15

Arjuna: How can you live in a worldly social setting without becoming affected by worldliness?

Krishna: Because I have no selfish aspirations behind my deeds, *karma* never pollutes me.

Arjuna: And that would work for me, too?

Krishna: Yes. Anyone who acts without selfish aspiration is never shackled by worldliness. Since ancient times, those who desired enlightenment worked in this frame of mind; and you should certainly do the same.

16-17

Arjuna: I still find it very confusing to grasp that performing *karma* can free me from *karma*.

Krishna: Even the experts find the subject of *karma* deep and difficult to comprehend. What is *karma* and what is *not*? Now I will erase all your misfortune by explaining this clearly.

Karma has three types: good *karma* (right action), bad *karma* (wrong action), and non-*karma* (inaction).

18

Arjuna: The first two types are not difficult to understand. *Right action* is to be dutifully responsible, and *wrong action* is to be irresponsible. What is *inaction*?

Krishna: Inaction can exist within action, and action can exist within inaction. When you become wise enough to see this, you can achieve *inaction* even in your worldly deeds.

19

Arjuna: Action and inaction are opposites. How can one exist within the other???

Krishna: If you to cast out selfish motivation from your deeds, the fire of your wisdom consumes those actions. They become *"inaction."*

20-21

Arjuna: But how can I give up selfish motivations?

Krishna: When you are satisfied within your own soul you will become independent of all needs. Then you will have no selfish ambitions left to fulfill. In such a state of mind you can never engage in worldly actions, even if you seem to be busy in so many ways.

When you give up selfish pursuits, your clear mind will come under your control. Then you will see that it is only your body doing things. You are 'inactive' – unimplicated in worldly reactions.

22-23

Arjuna: Anyone can say, "I don't desire anything, it is merely my body doing all these things." How do we know we are being sincere?

Krishna: If you are sincerely inactive you will be satisfied by whatever destiny provides, and thus will see success and failure as equal accomplishments. Then you will never be implicated in the worldliness of your deeds.

When your mind operates in clarity and knowledge you will naturally abandon selfish motives. Then your work becomes a sacred sacrifice, dissolving your *karmas* and granting enlightenment.

24

Arjuna: How is it possible that worldly deeds can have spiritual effects?

Krishna: In a sacrifice, *everything* becomes spiritual: the oil is spiritual, the fire is spiritual, the utensils are spiritual, the priest is spiritual, and the offerings are spiritual. Anything thoroughly involved in spirit becomes spiritual.

25-31

Arjuna: But I am not asking about a sacrificial ritual, I am asking about worldly deeds.

Krishna: Sacrifice is not just a ritual! There are many ways to make sacrifice: Some sacrifice rituals into the fire of spirituality. Others carefully sacrifice to the gods. Some sacrifice sense perception into the fire of restrictions. Others sacrifice the sense objects into the fires of the senses. Still others, illuminated by knowledge, sacrifice all their senses and even their breath into the fire of self-control.

All of them submit to strict vows; it's merely the form of their sacrifice that differs, not the substance. Some sacrifice wealth; others, austerities; others, deeds; still others sacrifice by studying philosophy. Some sacrifice their very breath, arresting it by offering exhalation to the fire of inhalation and visa-versa. Others cease inhalation altogether and offer exhalation into itself.

All of them understand "sacrifice." All of them are purified by sacrifice, enjoy the immortal nectar resulting from it, and attain the eternal spirit. But, my friend, those who don't understand sacrifice gain nothing in this world or the next.

32-33

Arjuna: Where are all these sacrifices explained?

Krishna: In the Vedas, "the mouthpiece of spirit." The important thing to understand is that they *all* involve work. Understand that and you will be emancipated.

Arjuna: Then, *any* work can be a "sacrifice"?

Krishna: It is the *wisdom* within the work which enables selflessness, which is spiritual. The work itself is not very important.

Arjuna: Why are there so many forms of sacrifice?

Krishna: Because there are so many different types of people. The external form of sacrifice is not very important; it is merely the catalyst to ignite the real fire of sacrifice: wisdom.

34

Arjuna: What is the best way to get wisdom?

Krishna: Respect wise people who have true vision. They will impart wisdom to you when you attentively inquire from all angles.

35

Arjuna: What will I see when I gain wisdom from those who see the truth?

Krishna: You will see that all living beings are within you, and that you are within me. You will never again fall into confusion.

36-38

Arjuna: But I am a very wicked person. I am a warrior and kill so many people. Can even I hope to attain this spiritual vision?

Krishna: Wisdom is a boat that will carry even the heaviest of the heinously wicked across the ocean of misery. Wisdom is a raging fire that burns wickedness to ash, as if it were dry wood. Nothing in this world could possibly be as purifying as wisdom. Follow the yoga of sacrifice to its final end and you will eventually enjoy this wisdom within your own soul.

39

Arjuna: But am I *qualified* to follow this yoga to its perfection?

Krishna: *Anyone* who puts their heart into it attains true wisdom.

Arjuna: What does it mean to "put my heart into it"?

Krishna: Make it more important than anything else, and therefore curtail all other endeavors. Trust that it will be *worth* it, for when you attain wisdom, you will very quickly attain the supreme peace.

Don't doubt this! Fools who have no conviction in the value of wisdom are ruined by their own doubts. Such bewildered people find no happiness here or hereafter. But a person who cuts through the bondage of doubts with knowledge can follow this yoga to its perfection, and renounce all selfish action. Then *karma* cannot bind him, Arjuna, for he is situated in his soul.

Therefore grasp the weapon of wisdom and slice through the doubts born of ignorance that have crowded your heart! On the strength of this wisdom, arise and stand firm, Arjuna!

~ 5 ~

ACTING IN WISDOM

1

Arjuna: Krishna! First you say "renounce karma," then you say "engage in karma wisely." Which one is better? Please tell me plainly!

2

Krishna: You can renounce action, or you can perform wise action - *both* lead to the ultimate goal. Between the two, however, wise action is better.

3-7

Arjuna: Why?

Krishna: Because it is easier.

Actually, the dichotomy between philosophical renunciation and wise action is a false one. Only a fool thinks that philosophy is different from wise action; the learned never say such things. You can achieve neither without striving for both, for the goal of philosophy is attained by action!

"Philosophy and action are two aspects of the same thing." That is the right way to see it.

Practical renunciation means being free from duality: neither desiring nor detesting anything. People who practice this are happy and completely liberated from the bondage inherent in worldly deeds. But, my friend, renunciation without practical application is a very miserable effort.

Put philosophy into practice and you will attain the spiritual goal easily. That's why I say: philosophy and action are both important, but *wise action*, their synthesis, is best.

8-14

Arjuna: How can I tell the difference between "wise action" and ordinary worldly deeds?

Krishna: A truly wise actor is a very pure soul. You have control of your mind and senses, and you treat all living beings as dearly as you treat yourself. Such a person is never bound by karmic reactions.

The active philosopher thinks: "seeing, hearing, touching, smelling, or tasting; walking or sleeping; breathing or talking; letting go or holding on; opening or closing... all of these are just natural, intrinsic reactions between senses and sense objects. I myself never truly do anything."

He thus invests all his actions with spiritual philosophy and divests his deeds of all self-centeredness. Karmic reaction cannot besmear such a person, just as water cannot dampen a lotus leaf.

The body, mind, intelligence, and senses of this *"karma-yogi"* are thus purified by renouncing all self-centeredness.

By renouncing selfish objectives, we achieve unwavering peace through our wise deeds. Without this wisdom, however, people are addicted to their own objectives, work for their own selfish whims, and thus become bound in karma.

It is said:

She dwells within the "City of Nine Gates" but knows that nothing done in that city is done by her or for her. She is the steward of that city, but she does not own any of its property, nor does she initiate the functions of its "citizens," nor does she have any claim to the results they create. Everything moves as a result of its own inherent nature. Knowing this, the self-controlled soul loses selfish interest in her deeds, and happily becomes renounced.[i]

15

Arjuna: Things happen as a result of "inherent natures," not divine will?

---

[i] This is a reference to one of the most philosophical Vedic texts, Śvetāśvatara Upanishad. The 'City of Nine Gates' is the human body with two eyes, two nostrils, two ears, a mouth, anus, and genital.

Krishna: No. Divine will does not cause good or bad things to happen. Fools cause such things, because ignorance has eclipsed their wisdom.

16

Arjuna: Are the fools doomed?

Krishna: No, they can cease being foolish. When wisdom finally rises like the sun, it destroys the inner darkness of ignorance and illuminates a higher path. It enlightens their thoughts, their soul, their attention, and their objectives. It washes away all confusion and ushers them to the supreme revelation.

17-19

Arjuna: When they attain such enlightenment, what do they become?

Krishna: They become very humble and learned. They see equality everywhere: in the teacher, the cow, the elephant, the dog, and even the dog-eater. They overcome the material world, right in the here-and-now. Because their mind is grounded in equality, they become as flawless and natural as spirit itself. They are already in the spiritual world.

20-21

Arjuna: What is their character?

Krishna: Beloved things do not thrill them. Hated things do not upset them. Their intellect is immovable and foolproof: for it understands and exists within spirit. They have no hunger for the touch of external things, because they delight in the pleasures within themselves. Their souls enjoy the infinite delight of union with the spirit.

22

Arjuna: They really have no interest in normal external sensual pleasures?

Krishna: They are intelligent, Arjuna! Why should they have any interest in "enjoyment" that begins and ends, and therefore is ultimately only the mother of misery?

23-26

Arjuna: What happens to them when they die?

Krishna: They do not wait for an afterlife. They immediately become very happy people, because they can forego the impulses that would lead to the pain of greed and anger. Their happiness is within. Their pleasures are within. They are illuminated from within! Thus they attain the flawless experience of spiritual *nirvāṇa*, and become spiritual.

In that spiritual condition, they work for the welfare of every living being. They are without any greed or anger, and are in complete control of their own will. When they die they will certainly continue in spiritual *nirvāṇa*.

27-28

Arjuna: When dying, what is the final practice by which they obtain such an exalted goal?

Krishna: When preparing to die, those who are already liberated shut out and keep distant from all unnecessary perceptions. They focus their eyes between their eyebrows. They exhale and inhale through their nose in a measured manner. Their wise senses, emotions, and thoughts are fixed upon enlightenment - giving up all other intentions, fears, and frustrations.

29

Arjuna: What "enlightenment" are they fixed upon attaining?

Krishna: Me. They seek the peace that comes from knowing me to be the true enjoyer of all their endeavors and efforts - the supreme god of all beings, and everyone's only true sweetheart!

~ 6 ~

YOGA AND MEDITATION

1

Arjuna: Who is a *real* "yogi," a real "renunciate"?

Krishna: Just having no roof over your head doesn't make you a renunciate. Merely having no job doesn't make you a yogi. You can be a real yogi and renunciate if you responsibly carry out your duties without regard for the pleasure or displeasure they bring you.

2-3

Arjuna: So, there is no significant difference between a yogi and a renunciate?

Krishna: They are the same. You can't be a yogi unless you renounce your selfish motivations. You can't renounce selfish motivations unless you are purified by practicing the yoga of selfless work.

The yoga of selfless work is the initial stage of renunciation. Once purified by this yoga, you no longer *need* to perform any duties.

4

Arjuna: What would be a sure sign that I have been purified and no longer require my active duties?

Krishna: You will feel no urges to endeavor for any sensual pleasure.

5-6

Arjuna: Once I attain such an elevated stage and cease from all ordinary activities, how would I continue to evolve - what would be my duty?

Krishna: At this stage you will deal directly with your mind. The mind tends to be the enemy of spiritual evolution - degrading us into selfish habits, but at this stage you will work to take full control of it and transform it into a friend, a spiritual inspiration.

7-9

Arjuna: What is it like to have control over the mind?

Krishna: You will always feel very peaceful, being in touch with the divine soul - regardless of external situations like cold or heat, happiness or distress, honor or dishonor. All your inner hungers will be understood and satisfied. You will dwell at the core of your being and be unaffected by sensual tribulations.

You will come to see that everything is the same: gold is just another rock; money, just paper. Eventually you will see people like this, too, having equal regard for sweethearts, relatives, neutrals, mediators, and opponents. You will not distinguish between friends and enemies, pious and sinful.

10

Arjuna: You said that my duty at this stage would be to directly work on transforming my mind. How would I do that?

Krishna: Meditation - the endeavor to control the flow of thoughts and not come under their grip.

Arjuna: How would I direct the flow of my thoughts?

Krishna: Direct them within your inner being, away from selfish desires and attachments. You must practice this in quiet seclusion.

11-12

Arjuna: Please say more about the proper place to practice meditation.

Krishna: Besides being secluded, it should be a sanctified place. When you find such a spot, make a place to sit.

Arjuna: How should I make the seat?

Krishna: Make it out of *kuśa* grass covered with deerskin, again covered by cloth. Elevate it a bit off the ground, but not too high. Sit there with good, steady posture, and practice directing the flow of your thoughts to a single point, curtailing your external sensual activities. This will make your soul very clear.

13-14

Arjuna: Can you elaborate on "steady posture"?

Krishna: Hold your torso, neck, and head straight, balanced, firm, and steady.

Arjuna: What about "curtailing the senses"?

Krishna: Restrain your perception from wandering here and there; focus your eyes on the tip of your nose and don't look elsewhere.

Arjuna: And controlling the "flow of the mind," how is that done?

Krishna: Let your thoughts pursue no lusts, especially not sexual lusts. Then you will be peaceful. You must also keep the mind from focusing on fears. Then your mind will come under your control.

Arjuna: When my mind is very clear and under my control, what should I do with it?

Krishna: Seat me within your pure mind! Make me your ultimate goal.

15

Arjuna: If I do this successfully, what will happen to me?

Krishna: If you dedicate your heart and soul constantly and regularly to this practice, you will attain the supreme peace, *nirvāṇa*, and come to my position.

16-17

Arjuna: Do you have any general advice on how to practice successfully?

Krishna: Don't eat too much, but don't starve either. Don't sleep too much, but don't stay up all the time either. Be intelligent in how you eat, relax, work, sleep, and stay awake. Then yoga will not be painfully difficult.

18-23

Arjuna: When is the path of yoga complete?

Krishna: The path is complete when your thoughts are fully under your control and thus remain fixed within the soul, freed from all selfish desires - like a candle in a windless place, never wavering from its inward focus.

The path of yoga is complete when you have stopped the outward flow of your thoughts and direct them inward towards your soul, experiencing the satisfaction of truly seeing your *self*.

This vision is so limitlessly, transcendentally delightful that you will never wander off from its reality. Gaining it, you will want for nothing else. Sheltered within it, not even the most severe suffering can disturb you. Comprehending it, your union with misery will dissolve, and your union with reality will solidify.

24-25

Arjuna: How do I begin the path of yoga?

Krishna: Begin with strong conviction: deep determination to practice it wholeheartedly. Then you can gradually give up all the conviction you had for selfish desires. This will enable you to more constantly and thoroughly discipline your mind and senses. Gradually your intelligence will become very strong and take full control of your emotional, impulsive mind - investing all thoughts and emotions within your soul, and never even considering anything else.

26

Arjuna: But when I attempt to fix the mind within myself, it wanders.

Krishna: It will wander here and there at first, because it is a restless and unsteady thing. Wherever it goes, bring it back and place it again under your control.

27-28

Arjuna: It is a monumental effort.

Krishna: For a monumental gain.

Arjuna: What gain?

Krishna: You will become one with pure spirit, unobscured by materialism, and completely free. You will gain the utmost happiness within your radiantly peaceful heart.

29

Arjuna: Where does this happiness come from?

Krishna: By casting off impurity, you come into constant union with soul, immersed in the bliss of Spirit's unlimited caress.

30

Arjuna: How can I have "constant union with soul" while I am still in this material world?

Krishna: You will see spirit in everything, and everything in spirit. Everywhere you look, you will see the same thing: spirit.

31-32

Arjuna: What is this "spirit" you speak of?

Krishna: Me! Seeing that "spirit" you will see me! You will see me in everything, and everything in me. You will never lose touch with me, nor I with you! See me in everything and you will be singularly engaged in my devotion, always and everywhere. You will be a yogi always immersed in me.

A Simple Gītā

Then you will be what I consider to be the paramount yogi. You will treat all living things as dearly as your own self, feeling their happiness and sadness as if it were your own.

33-34

Arjuna: Krishna, slayer of evils, the yoga of equipoise that you describe seems impossible for me. I am too distracted and unsteady for it. My mind is very impatient, overpowering, distorted, and stubborn. O Krishna, I think it would be easier to control the wind than to control the flow of my thoughts.

35-36

Krishna: No doubt the mind's restlessness is very difficult to curb, my strong friend. But you can do it by *practice* and detachment. Without these, yoga is impossible; but with these you can attain success.

37-39

Arjuna: If I tried but failed, what then? Would I not be a failure in *both* a worldly and spiritual sense; like a piece of cloud torn off from the main cloudbank only to disappear altogether? That is my fear, Krishna. I don't think anyone other than you can completely destroy this doubt.

40

Krishna: Arjuna, if you make sincere effort in yoga, you will *never* face failure, neither in this world nor beyond. My dear, one who does good never attains ill.

41-43

Arjuna: Then what, exactly, would happen to me?

Krishna: If you die as an imperfect yogi you would first go to the realms of paradise. After spending many years there, you will again appear on Earth, but in a blessed and pure family, or even in a family of wise yogis. Ah, what a rare and valuable birth! It will then be natural to revive the spiritual intelligence you worked for in your previous incarnation, and continue further towards perfection.

44

Arjuna: Why would it be "natural" to again take up yoga in my next life?

Krishna: Your former practice will certainly magnetize you towards automatic curiosity about yoga. Thus you would quickly pass through all the scriptures.

45

Arjuna: What if I fail again?

Krishna: The process will continue, even if it takes several lifetimes. Eventually your endeavors will become very tenacious and all the faults that troubled your progress will be removed. Then you will attain perfection and the supreme goal.

46

Arjuna: What did you mean when you said, "You would quickly pass through all the scriptures"?

Krishna: Scripture are, for the most part, a collection of principles to regulate selfish deeds. You would quickly become better than that and move on to interest in philosophy and knowledge. Again, you would quickly assimilate the wisdom of scripture, and thus become a yogi, dedicating the flow of your thoughts to union with the spirit.

Arjuna: So, to be a yogi is best?

Krishna: Yes, a yogi is the best of all people. So try to be a yogi, Arjuna.

47

Arjuna: Of all yogis, which type is the best?

Krishna: In my opinion, the very best of all yogis is the one who sincerely loves me, seeking me within the core of his own self.

~ 7 ~

THE YOGA OF DIVINE LOVE

1

Arjuna: The yoga you just described seems extremely difficult.

Krishna: Yes it is, my friend, but there is another, far more certain way to attain yoga. Listen carefully, I will teach you how to absorb your mind in me by the power of emotional attachment.

2-3

Arjuna: Please explain everything about this, this is what I really want to know about!

Krishna: I will explain it *fully*. I won't stop until you fully understand and realize it. I will leave nothing unknown.

I am about to explain things to you that are very, very rarely understood. Out of thousands of people, does even one strive for perfection? Out of *thousands* of people who have *achieved* perfection, does even one know these truths about me?

4-6

Arjuna: I will pay careful attention. Please begin.

Krishna: I have two categories of energy: objects that are experienced and subjects that experience.

The world of perceptible objects is made of my eight inferior, separated energies: *earth, water, fire, air, space, mind, intellect,* and especially *ego.*[i]

Life-force itself is my superior energy. It is superior because it animates and utilizes the other energies.

Everything that exists comes from these two types of energy, and both of them come from me. So, ultimately, it is I who animate both of them. Everything comes from me, and everything returns to me.

7

Arjuna: Where do *you* come from? What animates *you*?

Krishna: My friend, nothing at all is beyond me!

Arjuna: You are the causeless cause of everything?

---

[i] Ego causes these energies to appear "separated" from Krishna.

Krishna: Yes. Everything rests on me, like a necklace of pearls rests on a thread.

8-12

Arjuna: How can we be more aware of the *thread*? How can we better perceive your underlying presence everywhere?

Krishna: When you taste pure water, remember that you taste me. When you see the light of the Moon and Sun, know that you see me. When you hear "Om" pervading the Vedic mantras, realize that you hear me.

My friend, I am the sound that vibrates space. I am the ambition that motivates mankind. I am the pure fragrance of the earth. I am the brilliance of fire. I am the eternal seed of all beings and all states of being.

I am the life of the living, the discipline of the disciplined, the intelligence of the intelligent, the power of the powerful, and the strength of the strong.

I am the power to forego desires and attachments for the sake of morality, yet I am also the power of lust!

Certainly *everything* made of goodness, passion, or ignorance comes from me. Yet I am not wholly contained within any of them!

13

Arjuna: This is a beautifully divine way to see the world. But why is it so difficult to see it this way?

Krishna: Because everyone is bewildered by the threefold qualities of illusion: clarity, ambition, and ignorance. Under their spell, no one can perceive the infinite that is above and beyond them: me.

14

Arjuna: How can we get free from this illusion?

Krishna: This threefold illusion is insurmountable because it is my own powerful energy. Only those who come to me for shelter can pass beyond it.

15

Arjuna: That doesn't seem so difficult. Why doesn't everyone do it?

Krishna: Many people are vile, villainous fools. Refusing me, they take shelter of their own dark character, because illusion has hijacked their "knowledge."

16

Arjuna: What types of people *do* seek your shelter?

Krishna: Four types of good people: the needy, the curious, the ambitious, and the wise.

17

Arjuna: Among them, who achieves your shelter most fully?

Krishna: The wise are very special because they always come to me exclusively out of love.[i] I am beloved to the wise, and the wise are beloved to me!

18-19

Arjuna: Are the others not also dear to you?

Krishna: They are all special, but the wise soul is as dear to me as my own self. The wise are grounded in spiritual union with me, and achieve the very highest goal.

Such a great soul is very rare! Only after many births does one become wise and seek my shelter, knowing that, "Vāsudeva is all there is."

20

Arjuna: Why are the others not as dear to you?

Krishna: They have ulterior motives. So, they are distracted to ulterior shelters, under the sway of their own desires.

Arjuna: They will worship other gods, other beings, other things?

Krishna: Yes.

---

[i] The definition of wisdom is not scholarship but *"eka-bhakti"* - pure love without ulterior motive.

21-22

Arjuna: Are you jealous?

Krishna: No, I *help* them achieve their ulterior motives! I give them the firm faith to dedicate themselves to whomever or whatever they are inspired towards. Taking that faith, they worship whatever or whomever they are inclined to worship and fulfill their selfish desires. I completely facilitate all of this.

23

Arjuna: In the end, do they finally take shelter of you?

Krishna: No, because their meager intelligence doesn't perceive my hand in any of this. They are simply obsessed with their temporary objectives. Thus, those who worship other gods go to other gods. Only those who singularly love me come to me.

24

Arjuna: What about the "curious"? Why are they not as dear to you as the wise?

Krishna: They tend to think that I am merely a "manifestation of the unmanifest." They do not understand that I *personally* am infinite and unsurpassed.

25-26

Arjuna: If you are everything you say you are, wouldn't it be obvious to everyone?

Krishna: I do not exhibit myself to the masses! Fools eclipse themselves by their union with illusion. They are incapable of perceiving that I am beginningless and infinite.[i]

I know the past, present and future of them all, but none of them knows me at all!

27

Arjuna: At what point did the living entity lose awareness of you?

Krishna: From the very beginning, Arjuna! As soon as they were created they experienced the duality of selfish desire and repulsion, from which illusion arises, and by which all living beings are intoxicated.

28-30

Arjuna: Then how does anyone manage to gain awareness of you?

Krishna: Illusion's misfortunes gradually end when someone is responsible and dutiful. As illusion subsides they become free from duality and very intent upon getting free from things like old age and

---

[i] When souls desire of their own accord to comprehend Krishna, then he begins to reveal himself. Until that time, he stays out of the way of our precious illusions.

death. Thus they begin to desire a loving relationship with me

They come to fully understand *spirit*, *soul*, and *karma* - and perceive that I am the essential reality of every *object*, every *divinity*, and every *effort*. Their thoughts become united with me, even up to the moment of death.

~ 8 ~

CHOOSE YOUR AFTERLIFE

1-2

Arjuna: You just mentioned *spirit, soul,* and *karma*. What does each term really mean? You also mentioned the essential reality of every *object, divinity,* and *effort*. What are these?[i]

You also mentioned that devoted souls attain the highest destination by being aware of you at the time of death. Can you explain this more thoroughly?

---

[i] The Sanskrit terms for these six items in question are, in order, *brahman, adhi-ātma, karma, adhi-bhūta, adhi-daiva,* and *adhi-yajña*.

3-4

Krishna:

Spirit   is the supreme indestructible energy.

Soul   is the inherent essence of what you are.

Karma   creates the causes behind
every situation that comes into being.

The essential reality of every object
is to disappear.

The essential nature of all divinities
is the Original Person.

The essence of all efforts
is me, the soul of all souls.

5-6

Arjuna: Can you also respond to the last question, about how devoted souls attain the highest destination by being aware of you at the time of death?

Krishna: Whatever state of mind you are in at the end of one lifetime determines the type of existence you attain in the next. So, if you remember me in the final moments of casting off your body, you will attain my own nature, without a doubt.

7-8

Arjuna: So, I can think of anything and everything throughout my life, but if by chance I think of you at the time of death...

Krishna: That's impossible.

Arjuna: Why?

Krishna: At the moment of death only spontaneous, unstoppable thoughts will fill your mind. If you wish to attain me by remembering me at *that* moment, you must practice doing so throughout *every* moment of your life. Enwrap your mind and intellect in me by living your life according to my instructions. Then you will attain me.

Have no doubt about it. If you practice uniting your thoughts to me, without wandering to other topics, your thoughts will carry you to the Paramount Divine Person.

9-10

Arjuna: How should I practice thinking about you?

Krishna: Contemplate the divine qualities of the Paramount Person. He is ingenious, ancient, the leader of all, subtler than sub-atomic particles, the maintainer of everyone, amazingly beautiful, radiant like the sun, and beyond all darkness.

Invest the power from your breathing into the area between your eyebrows, and keep these divine contemplations in your mind always, up till the very end. This yogic meditation will be very powerful because it is empowered by devotion. It will take you to the Paramount Person.

11-13

Arjuna: I want to know more about this practice.

Krishna: Alright, I will summarize for you the spiritual practices followed by mystics who abandon all other desires, to exclusively strive for entrance into what the wise describe as "imperishable."

First you must take full control of all your senses - closing the "doorways" to the external world. Then, confine your thoughts within your heart and focus the consciousness in your breath towards the top of your head.

While contemplating me, vibrate this single spiritual syllable: "Om." If you can continue this practice even while casting off your body you will attain the topmost goal.

14

Arjuna: What is the essence of this practice?

Krishna: Always remember me with constant, undivided attention. If you do this, my friend, you will gain me quite easily.

15

Arjuna: What happens then?

Krishna: When you achieve me, you will never again achieve another birth in this house of suffering and impermanence. Your soul will blossom into the fullest perfection of the topmost achievements.

16

Arjuna: What's wrong with taking another birth? For example, a birth in heaven?

Krishna: Every heaven up to and including Brahmā's is a place from which you must again return. But when you come to me, Arjuna my cousin, you will never know another birth.

17-19

Arjuna: But many people think that heaven is eternal and that Brahmā never dies.

Krishna: Maybe, but the wise know that Brahmā's day lasts for a thousand ages, and so does his night. When his day begins, all the creatures of the world become manifest. When his night begins, they all dissolve and de-manifest. Again and again they dissolve with his dusk and awaken with his dawn.

Arjuna: Does he ever die?

Krishna: Yes, and with him the entire creation dissolves.[i]

---

[i] A full day and night in Brahmā's heaven is equivalent to the experience of 24 million earthly years, or, by another opinion, 8 billion 640 million years. Brahmā's lifespan - synonymous with the lifespan of the universe is either 864 billion or 311 trillion and 40 billion earthly years (depending on the method of calculation).

20

Arjuna: What is beyond all this?

Krishna: Beyond Brahmā and his destructible universe is an eternal, indestructible, non-material reality. It is never destroyed, even when everything else is annihilated.

21

Arjuna: If it is beyond Brahmā, who is the lord of that realm?

Krishna: That famous place - the imperishable, non-material, supreme destination from which no one departs - is my supreme abode!

22

Arjuna: How can I attain it?

Krishna: Arjuna, that Supreme Person in his supreme abode is attained only by love! Not just any love, but *pure* love – without any ulterior motive.

Arjuna: What inspires such purity of love, undeviated to any other person or thing?

Krishna: When you realize that the Supreme Person is within the core of everyone, permeating everything, how would it be possible for your love to be diverted to any other person or thing?

23-27

Arjuna: Can you say a little more about the "destination from which no one strays"?

Krishna: I will describe the two paths by which departed spiritualists move towards and away from that imperishable destination.

The path which leads to that spiritual destination takes one passed the gods of fire, light, daytime, the waxing moon, and the northerly sun. The path that leads back comes from the lunar heavens and takes one passed the gods of smoke, night, the waning moon, and the southerly sun. So, there have always been two paths for the departed soul: a bright one and a dark one. The bright path leads towards the spiritual goal from which there is no return. The dark path takes one back to rebirth.

A spiritualist who knows these two paths is never thwarted.

28

Arjuna: It seems there are many details.

Krishna: Maybe, but the essence is this: Just try to unite your heart to mine. That is all you really need to do to be a yogi and attain the original, paramount abode - surpassing all the best results obtainable on *any* path of philosophy, ritual, austerity, or charity!

~ 9 ~

KRISHNA IS EVERYTHING

1-2

Krishna: Now I will tell you the *most* intimate of all my secrets, which only my friends can truly understand. Learn this, and you will be liberated from all misfortune. It is the supreme science, the monarch of mysteries, the purest purifier - uniquely enjoyable, self-evident, and everlasting.

3

Arjuna: Why should something so enjoyable and beneficial be so secret?

Krishna: Because common men have little interest in it. They are not interested in attaining me. Instead they want some temporary paradisiac from which they soon return to the cycle of mortality.

4-5

Arjuna: What are these most confidential secrets?

Krishna: It begins here:

I am spread throughout this entire universe, in an imperceptible form. Everything is in me, but I am not contained within anything. And so, everything is not me.

Arjuna: What? This is almost incomprehensible.

Krishna: That is the mystic nature of my being!

Arjuna: Can you explain more clearly?

Krishna: I am the original entity from which everything comes. I support everyone and everything, but I am not contained within anyone or anything.

6

Arjuna: It is still very difficult to understand. Can you give an analogy?

Krishna: Yes: The atmosphere is contained within space, and space is within the atmosphere. But the atmosphere does not contain space.[i]

---

[i] Everything is contained within space; similarly, everything exists within Krishna. Space is also within everything; similarly, Krishna exists within everything. Nothing can contain the whole of space; similarly nothing is wholly Krishna, except Krishna himself.

A Simple Gītā

7

Arjuna: I am beginning to understand. But, what about things that have been destroyed - do they also exist within you?

Krishna: Yes. When a thousand ages end, Arjuna, everything is destroyed and becomes energy; *my* energy. When a new cycle of a thousand ages begins again, I recreate everything.

8

Arjuna: How do you recreate everything from energy?

Krishna: I create by placing living beings into my energy, which then automatically takes different forms in conformity to their will. Again and again I do this, cycle after cycle.

9

Arjuna: So you are not directly responsible for the things that arise in the world? The direct cause of the things that exist in the world is the will of the living entities?

Krishna: That's right. I am a neutral party in all this, never implicated in the causality of their selfish deeds.

10

Arjuna: What role does a "neutral party" play in the universe?

Krishna: I keep my glance upon it and thereby grant it the power to reproduce all its mobile and immobile forms.

11

Arjuna: But here you are standing in front of me. How can *you* be the source and overseer of everything in the universe?

Krishna: Fools think that I am a limited being contained within a human body. You are not such a fool, Arjuna.

12

Arjuna: How do you know I am not?

Krishna: Because you are not like them.

Arjuna: What are they like?

Krishna: Those fools take shelter of the material world. Intoxicated by it they become ungodly, wild, and mindless. They develop useless ambitions, useless endeavors, and useless understandings.

13

Arjuna: I'm not like that?

Krishna: No, you are like the great souls.

Arjuna: What are they like?

Krishna: Great souls take shelter of the spiritual world and adore me without ulterior motive, because they understand that I am the inexhaustible origin of everything.

14

Arjuna: You've described their heart, what about their deeds?

Krishna: Those great souls always strive with determined commitment to constantly perform *kīrtana:* glorifying me and constantly offering me affectionate respect and worship.

15

Arjuna: Are there other ways to worship you?

Krishna: Yes. The not-so-great souls worship me indirectly in many different ways. They worship me as the effort to gain knowledge, as the oneness uniting plurality, and as the personification of the universe itself.

16-19

Arjuna: Why are these less wonderful than *kīrtana?*

Krishna: Because they distract from the essence and divert one's focus to external details.

Arjuna: What is the essence of all worship, from which one must not be distracted?

Krishna: I am.

I am the ritual. *I* am the sacrifice. *I* am the ancestor's offering. *I* am the sacred herb. *I* am the mantra. *I* am the oil, the fire and the offering. *I* am father, mother, provider, and grandfather. *I* am the objective of "*oṁ*," which purifies the knowledge in the Ṛg, Sāma, and Yajur Vedas. *I* am the goal, the husband, the lord, the witness, the home, the shelter, and the sweetheart. *I* am creation, destruction, and existence. *I* am the original seed. *I* am warmth. *I* withhold and send forth the rains. *I* am immortality and death. *I* am the real and unreal.

20

Arjuna: What becomes of those whose worship is distracted from the essence?

Krishna: Knowing only the external ways of rituals, they perform sacrifice with prayers to me that express the desire to enter paradise. Drinking the ritual Soma, they indeed become purified and enter the pure realm of the king of gods, where there they enjoy the gods' delights.

21

Arjuna: That sounds pretty good.

Krishna: Yes, but by enjoying the vast heavenly realm they eventually exhaust their piety and then must return to the world of mortals. So, birth and death is the end result of worship done for selfish rewards.

22

Arjuna: What becomes of those who truly worship you with pure selfless love, not distracted by selfish ulterior motives?

Krishna: I personally take care of them.

Arjuna: How?

Krishna: I protect them from whatever faults they have. And I make firm whatever virtues they possess.

23

Arjuna: You just said that you are everything. So if I worship anything, I worship you…

Krishna: Yes, but that is generally unbeknownst to those who worship many gods! They have faith in and devotion to such gods, unaware of the truth that they are actually worshipping me indirectly. So, this is not a recommended path.

24

Arjuna: What is the recommended path?

Krishna: To be aware that I am every sacrifice, every god, and every master - and therefore to directly worship me without distraction. People who are not aware of this become distracted by the many gods and rituals, and thus remain in the mortal realm.

25

Arjuna: What if one doesn't directly worship you, but worships the gods knowing that they are actually you?

Krishna: Why would they do that? They would worship me directly!

Worshippers of the gods attain the gods. Worshippers of ancestors attain the ancestors. Worshippers of spirits attain those spirits. But only those who directly worship me can attain me.

26

Arjuna: How should I directly worship you?

Krishna: It is simple, easy, and joyful: with love.

Arjuna: How should I express that love?

Krishna: Out of love, offer me a leaf, flower, fruit, or water. When these are offered lovingly by a devoted soul, I eagerly accept them.

27-28

Arjuna: These simple acts of pure love are undoubtedly beautiful. But, what if I cannot be so simple and pure?

Krishna: Then, my friend, *whatever* you do, whatever you eat, whatever sacrifices you make, whatever gifts you give, whatever difficulties you undertake... do them for my sake, not your own.

This discipline of renunciation will purify you completely from the positive and negative partiality of selfish deeds. Then you will be able to simply love me.

29-30

Arjuna: A devotee simply gives you a flower and attains the supreme destination - a non-devotee performs elaborate, difficult ceremonies and attains nothing but the cycle of mortality... Why are you so partial towards your devotee and indifferent towards those who are distracted from loving you?

Krishna: I am not partial to anyone!!! I am equal to everyone! I neither favor nor disfavor anyone. But anyone who shows me true devotion keeps me in their heart... so, naturally, they are also in my heart!

I am open to everyone and anyone. Even if someone has been a very foul person, if they somehow develop love for me without ulterior motive I consider them a saint, and very righteous.

31

Arjuna: How can a very foul person have pure love for you?

Krishna: They don't remain foul! This love immediately makes them pure and righteous, granting them spiritual peace! My dear cousin, you should declare that one who loves me will never fail to become righteous!

32

Arjuna: So anyone and everyone can become your devotee?

Krishna: Yes, even those born into foul circumstances, or those who are not very educated in spiritual matters. Everyone can attain the supreme destination by pure love for me.

33

Arjuna: What about those born into good circumstances?

Krishna: Of course! It is even easier for philosophical intellectuals and devoted philosopher-kings like you! *However* you may have come into this temporary and unhappy situation - through "good" or "bad" circumstances - you can always take up my pure devotional service!

34

Arjuna: What is the essence of such devotion?

Krishna: Become devoted to me by keeping me in your mind, working for my sake, and being respectful to me. With your soul thus dedicated to me, certainly you will attain me.

~ 10 ~

COMPREHENDING THE INCOMPREHENSIBLE

1

Arjuna: I am still not sure I understand what you said about you being the origin of everything, yet beyond everything…

Krishna: Arjuna, you are so dear to me. I only desire your well-being. So, I will again explain those supreme secrets about me.

2

Arjuna: I am sorry to make you repeat yourself.

Krishna: No, no. Everyone has a hard time comprehending what I am trying to explain. Even the gods and the greatest sages don't understand my origin. After all, I am the origin of *them*.

3

Arjuna: You are the origin of everything, but what is your origin?

Krishna [putting his hand on his chest]: I am the origin without an origin. Thus I am the supreme master of everything. If anyone understands this, they are liberated from all confusions and misfortune, even if they are the most ordinary mortal.

4

Arjuna: Why is it so confusing to comprehend a self-originating entity?

Krishna: Because the origin is beyond the limits of its emanations, beyond every facility you might use to comprehend it.

Arjuna: What about the tools of knowledge and science?

Krishna: I am above and beyond all of them: intelligence, knowledge, certainty, forbearance, realism, restraint, equipoise... Existence and non-existence and their associated fear and fearlessness...

5

Arjuna: What about mystical tools of understanding?

Krishna: I am above and beyond all these as well: non-violence, non-discrimination, desirelessness, austerity, charity, fame, or infamy...

6

Arjuna: You said that you are the origin of all the sages and gods, but some say they all come from Aditi.

Krishna: What do you think?

Arjuna: I know Aditi comes from Dakṣa, who comes from Brahmā. But I have also heard that all the sages and gods come from Brahmā.

Krishna: And what do you think of that?

Arjuna: I don't know. *You* please explain how everyone can come from you, yet so many people say that everything comes from Aditi, who comes from Brahmā.

Krishna: Brahmā is born from my thoughts. Then, from his thoughts come four great sages, and then seven more, and then the forefathers, from whom everyone else in the world is eventually born.

7-8

Arjuna: Alright, I accept that you are the cause of everything and everyone. Since that means you are above and beyond any tool of comprehension possessed by your emanations, but my question is how can anyone *ever* comprehend you?

Krishna: Through *devotion*. When you just begin to comprehend my mystical nature, you will develop a devotional feeling towards me, wanting to come closer and unite yourself to me. That is sure and certain.

He is the cause of all causes. Everything comes from him. If you understand this intelligently, you will start to feel very deep devotion towards me.

9

Arjuna: After developing some initial devotion towards you, what happens next?

Krishna: You will then seek out those whose thoughts are enrapt in me, whose very hearts beat for me. Finding them, you will further enlighten one another by always discussing me with great satisfaction and pleasure!

10

Arjuna: And then?

Krishna: When you are always on that loving path of adoration, I will empower you with supernatural intellect, capable of comprehending me.

11

Arjuna: What about my inherent ignorance, won't that interfere?

Krishna: No. I will personally ensure that your dark shadows of ignorance are dispelled by the brilliant light of knowledge.

12-13

Arjuna [standing up enthusiastically and gesturing dramatically]: "The supreme spirit, the supreme being, the supreme pure, the eternal divine person, the original divinity, unborn, and exceptional." All the sages like divine Nārada, Asita, Devala, and Vyāsa describe you thus; and now you yourself have explained it to me!

14-16

Krishna: Do you believe it?

Arjuna: Yes, my friend. I know that everything you say to me is the truth!

Krishna: Are you not disturbed by others who hold a different opinion of me?

Arjuna: Certainly not! No one amongst the godly or ungodly can comprehend how you manifest your all-attractive personality. Certainly only you are capable of understanding your own self – the Ultimate Person, the origin of everything, master of everything, divinity of divinity, and husband of the universe. There can be no doubt that *only* you are qualified to describe your infinite divine qualities... So please describe them now!

Krishna: If my qualities are infinite, how can I describe them?

Arjuna: At least describe those that are relevant and easily comprehensible, the qualities by which you pervade everything that we already experience.

17

Krishna: Why should I talk more about myself?

Arjuna: I need to know these things so I can always be enrapt in thoughts of you! You must explain, so that each and every thing I see will remind me of your All-Attractive self.

18

Krishna: But I have already said too much about myself!

Arjuna: I want to know in more detail about your mystical power and opulence. You can speak again and again about these things, but I will never feel that I have tasted enough of that nectar!

19-38

Krishna [very affectionately]: Yes, my dear. I will certainly tell you about my divine opulences, but since they expand beyond limit I will only speak of those that are very relevant.

I am the soul within everyone's heart.
I am the beginning, middle, and end of everything.

Among Aditi's divine children
I am Viṣṇu.

Among lights
I am the radiant sun.

Among storms
I am the fiercest wind.

Among stars
I am the Moon.

Among Veda [books]
I am Sāma Veda [songs].

Among gods
I am Indra.

Among the senses
I am the mind.

Among living things
I am the life-force.

Among Rudras
I am Śiva.

Among Yakṣas and Rākṣasas [powers of enjoyment]
I am Kuvera [the treasurer].

Among Vasus [primordial elements]
I am fire.

Among mountains
I am Meru.

Among great priests
I am the god's priest [Bṛhaspati].

Among generals
I am the god of war [Skanda].

Among pools
I am the ocean.

Among great sages
I am Bhṛgu.

Among sounds
I am the single syllable ["oṁ"].

Comprehending the Incomprehensible

Among sacrifices
I am the whispering of mantra.

Among immovable things
I am the Himalayas.

Among trees
I am the banyan.

Among heavenly sages
I am Nārada.

Among celestial musicians
I am Citraratha.

Among the perfected
I am the scholar Kapila.

Among horses
I am Uccaiḥśravā [the divine horse],
born from nectar.

Among elephants
I am Airāvata [Indra's elephant].

Among humans
I am the king.

Among weapons
I am lightning.

Among cows
I am the wish-fulfilling cow.

Among reasons to procreate
I am Cupid.

Among serpents
I am Vāsuki [king of dragons].

Among dragons

I am Ananta [Viṣṇu's dragon].

Among aquatic beings
I am Varuṇa [god of the celestial ocean].

Among the spirits who assist the departed
I am the friendly Aryamā.

Among those who enforce punishment
I am the god of death [Yama].

Among demons
I am Prahlāda.

Among restrictions
I am time.

Among animals
I am the lion.

Among birds
I am Garuḍa [the divine eagle].

Among purifiers
I am the wind.

Among warriors
I am Paraśurāma.

Among fish
I am the Capricorn.

Among rivers
I am the Ganges.

Among creations,
I am the beginning, the completion, *and* the process.

Among sciences
I am self-knowledge.

Comprehending the Incomprehensible

Among logics
I am the conclusion.

Among letters
I am "A".

Among compound words
I am the dual-compound.

Among things that endure
I am persistence.

Among creators
I am the many-headed [Brahmā].

Among thieves
I am death.

Among beginnings
I am birth.

Among women
I am fame, beauty, fine speech,
memory, intelligence, dedication, and forbearance.

Among the hymns of Sāma Veda
I am the Bṛhat-sāma.

Among poetic meters
I am *gāyatrī*.

Among months
I am the month of harvest [November].

Among seasons
I am the season of flowers [Spring].

Among cheaters
I am the gamble.

Among the winners
I am the power.

Among efforts
I am the victory.

Among the strong
I am the strength.

Among the Vṛṣṇi
I am Vāsudeva.

Among the Pāṇḍavas
I am Arjuna.

Among scholars
I am Vyāsa.

Among poets
I am Venus.

Among deterrents
I am punishment.

Among ambitions
I am morality.

Among secrets
I am silence.

Among the knowledgeable
I am knowledge.

39

Krishna: Whatever else there might be, I am the very essence of it. There is nothing, living or non-living, that can exist independently of me.

40-42

Arjuna: Go on!

Krishna: I must stop here, otherwise there is no limit to these divine opulences. All these examples I gave are merely metaphors pointing you towards my expansive opulence.

Whatever you encounter that is sublime, beautiful, and powerful, you must understand that it is just a product of a fragment of my splendor. So what is the point of making this list longer and longer? Simply understand that I pervade everything in the entire universe with just a single fragment of myself.

~ 11 ~

SEEING IT ALL

1-4

Arjuna: My dear friend, whose eyes are as wide as lotus leaves, you have lovingly explained the most confidential secrets about yourself, erasing all my confusions. I have *heard* of your endless grandeur as the beginning and end of all things. Now I would like to *see* it with my own eyes. If you think I am able, O master of all mysteries, please let me see that limitless, majestic form of the Ultimate Person.

5-7

Krishna: Yes, my friend, look upon my form, with hundreds upon thousands of divine, multifaceted colors and shapes.

Look upon the Āditya gods, who maintain the universe; the Vasu gods, who are the substances of the universe; the Rudra gods, who destroy the universe; the Aśvini gods, who give health and beauty; the Marut gods of storms; and so many other amazing things that have never been seen before!

See in me *the singularity* - the entire universe simultaneously situated in one place!

In this form of mine you will behold *everything* you wish to see!

8

Arjuna: I cannot see it!

Krishna: Of course you cannot see my mystic opulence with your ordinary eyes. So, I bestow divine vision to you!

9-14

Krishna then showed Arjuna his form of supreme majesty: Countless eyes and mouths, countless incredible sights, countless divine ornaments, countless divine weapons held aloft; dressed in divine clothing and flower necklaces, emitting divine fragrances; the brilliant divinity of absolutely astonishing wonder, the unlimited being whose face is everywhere.

If a thousand suns shone in the sky together, perhaps the brilliance might compare to the radiance of this great being. Within the body of that invisible god of gods Arjuna could see the universal singularity expanded infinitely.

Then, overcome by astonishment while his hair stood up on end, Arjuna folded his hands, bowed his head, and began to speak.

15-19

Arjuna: In your divine body I see the great master Śiva, Brahmā upon his lotus-seat, all the gods, and all the sages and supernatural serpents. I see *everything* there, in all detail and specificity.

I see countless arms, bellies, mouths, and eyes. I see your limitless form everywhere. I see no end, no middle, and no beginning in you; the master of everything; the form of everything.

Everywhere I see crowns, maces, and discs brilliant with powerful splendor. It is difficult to look upon this radiance, brighter than the blazing sun.

I must conclude that you are the paramount, imperishable goal of philosophy. You are the ultimate root of the entire universe. You are the untiring sustainer of its eternal laws and principles. You are the ever-enduring Person.

Your limitless power is without beginning, middle, or end. Your arms are endless. The moon and sun are your eyes. I see brilliant fire, ignited by your own potency, radiating from your mouth and heating the universe.

20

Universal Form: Now behold another, more savage side of the divine universe...

Arjuna: The bewildering sight of you in this primal and savage form disturbs the gods, humans, and demons. From outer space down to the earth, and in all directions in between, I see only you, O great soul.

21

Universal Form: It disturbs the gods and human sages?

Arjuna: Yes. Hosts of gods enter into you, some of them fearfully putting their palms together while petitioning you. Hosts of the greatest sages and mystics declare, "Let there be well-being," as they recite to you the hymns and prayers of the Vedas.

22

Universal Form: Who exactly do you see among these gods?

Arjuna: The destroying Rudras, the maintaining Ādityas, the fundamental Vasus, the perfected Sādhyās, the universal Viśvas, the two beautiful Aśvini, the stormy Maruts; even the ancestral Pitṛ, the best among the angelic Gandharva, the wealthy Yakṣa, and the dangerous Asura; certainly *everyone* beholds you in awe.

23-25

Universal Form: And you? Are you also perturbed by awe?

Arjuna: Like everyone else, I am disturbed by seeing you in this huge form, with so many mouths, eyes, powerful arms, thighs, feet, stomachs, and frightening teeth; touching the sky, radiating countless colors, with gaping mouths and wide, glaring eyes. Seeing you like this perturbs me to the core of my being. O Viṣṇu, I have lost my composure and balance!

Your frightening teeth and faces seem just like the fires of doom. I can discover no peace or prosperity in any direction. O master of gods, oh refuge of the world, be kind to me!

26-31

Universal Form: Now behold in me the future! Look at the outcome of this war? What do you see?

Arjuna: Everyone in the opposing army - its leader, its most heroic champions, and all of our foremost warriors, too - all are rushing into your mouths, to be crushed by your terribly frightening teeth. I see some of them stuck with heads smashed between those teeth.

Like moths rushing full-speed into the brilliant blaze of a flame, or like multitudes of rivers rushing to be consumed by the waves of the ocean, all the heroes of mankind rush to their destruction in your blazing mouths.

O Viṣṇu, your blazing tongues seize and devour everyone, from all directions. Your power reaches beyond the world, which is scorched by your terrible rays.

Respectfully, I ask you to please be merciful, O greatest god, and explain this horrible form. I want to understand your motive, and incomprehensible objective. *Who are you?*

32-34

Universal Form: I am time, pushing forward the doom of fate; the ultimate destroyer of everything.

Arjuna: What is your mission?

Universal Form: My objective is to destroy this entire world. I will destroy the warriors on both sides of the battle… except for you. Therefore, arise! Conquer your enemies and gain your famous and fortunate kingdom. Because of their past deeds, it is *I* who have truly destroyed all of them. Just become instrumental in this, O great archer.

I have already destroyed all the heroic warriors: your guru, your grandfather, your wife's kidnapper, your mortal enemy, and everyone else. So defeat them without worry. Merely fight, and your enemies will fall.

35-36

Arjuna folds his trembling hands, fearfully bows, and in a faltering voice addresses his now unseen friend, Krishna.

Arjuna: O Master of the Senses, hearing your *kīrtana* makes the whole world joyful and delighted.

Krishna: But you have just seen my horrible, and fearsome aspect! How can you still be cognizant of my joyful and delightful features?

Arjuna: Your ghastly form exists only for the sake of ghastly people - who flee from it in terror. The perfected souls do not flee, they offer you respect in all circumstances, fearsome or pleasant.

37

Krishna: Why should they respect something so horrible?

Arjuna: Because it is also a part of you, who are never *truly* destructive. You are the original creator of the creator. You are the limitless master of the benevolent gods. You are the shelter of the universe.

Krishna: But I *can* be truly destructive! This form I am showing you proves it.

Arjuna: This destructive form is nothing but a reflection of *our own* destructive nature. You yourself are far beyond the relative good and bad of these temporary causes and effects.

38

Krishna: What do you mean? Am I beyond these horrific affairs, or am I within them?

Arjuna: This universe exists within you, but you are far beyond it - *transcendent*. You are the original, most ancient Divine Being. You are everything that we comprehend, and you are also comprehension itself, and you are also the state of being that transcends both. You are the unlimited being pervading everything that exists.

39-40

Krishna: Ah. That is why great souls always offer me respect, even amidst a horrific universe? But wouldn't it be wiser to respect someone else?

Arjuna: "Someone else"? But who is *not* you or your energy? You are airy Vāyu. You are deathly Yama. You are fiery Agni. You are spacious Varuṇa. You are the heavenly bodies like the Moon. You are the original ancestor, Brahmā. So who should we respect more than you!?

Let there be respect after respect unto you, a thousand times over, and even that is not enough! Still more I should again offer respect after respect to you! I bow to you from the front and the back. You are everything, so let me bow to you always and everywhere!

Krishna: What is all this reverence? Am I not simply your *friend* - standing in your chariot, right in front of you?

Arjuna: Your limitless power and unstoppable force support everything. In that sense, you are everything.

41-42

Krishna: Answer directly. Am I your friend or not?

Arjuna: I took you as my friend, revealing just how full of self-importance I am. Ignorant of your true greatness I chatted with you like a brother, "Hey Krishna! Hey cousin! Hey friend!"

Krishna: But that was because of your love for me!

Arjuna: Maybe, but I even criticized you in sarcastic jokes while we relaxed together, lying or sitting around and eating together as if we were equals. O Inscrutable One, I ask your forgiveness for my countless transgressions.

43-44

Krishna: Don't talk like this! Everything you have ever done for me was done out of *love!*

Arjuna: Then please forgive me, as a loving father excuses the behavior of his children. After all, you really are the father of everything animate and inanimate in the world. You are the most worshipable and glorious guru. How can there be anyone else like you? How can anyone amongst humans, demons, or gods be equal with your infinite power?

Therefore please be patient with me, like a guru or a father. Forgive me like a friend forgives a friend - like a lover forgives the beloved.

45-46

Krishna: All right, but what will become of the relationship we had?

Arjuna: Let us return to it! I am thrilled to have seen this never-before-seen sight – yet it has cast my mind into the waves of fear. Please return to your form as the compassionate master of gods, and shelter of the world.

O thousand-armed universal form, I hope to see you in your four-armed form, with a mace and disc in your hands, and a crown upon your head.

47-50

Krishna: Happily, I used my mystic power to give you the vision of that unsurpassed form of mine: powerful, universal, endless, and beginningless. No one but you has seen all this before in such detail.

Arjuna, that form cannot be seen on the strength of sacrifice, philosophical study, charitable deeds, scrupulous duties, nor even by the most severe austerities. Comprehending that form allows one to see me even in the normal affairs of the everyday world. None but you have seen it so well.

But this terrifying universal form has disturbed and confused you, and that was not my intention. So now be freed from this fear, and regain your affectionate, loving disposition towards me.

51

Krishna then withdrew Arjuna's perception of the staggering Universal Form and showed himself in the more human-like four-armed Viṣṇu form as he transitioned back into his original, gentle form as Krishna. Arjuna breathed a sigh of relief...

Arjuna: Dear Krishna, seeing you again in your gentle, human form calms my mind and allows me to return to my natural state.

52-53

Krishna: The form you see me in *now* is the rarest of all visions. Even the gods constantly aspire for a vision of *this* form.

By studying scriptures, by undergoing austerities, by giving everything away, or by worship - it is impossible by any of these means to see me in the form you now see.

54

Arjuna: Then how am I seeing it?

Krishna: Because you have pure, undivided love for me! Arjuna, that is the only way I can be known in this form, as Krishna.

Arjuna: But everyone here on the battlefield can see you, too.

Krishna: They do not truly see me. Only by undivided love can one enter into comprehension of the full truth of what you now see before you.

55

Arjuna: How can people like those around us also gain this sweet vision?

Krishna: If they work for my sake, make me their ultimate objective, give their love to me, cast off all other embraces, and never think of any creature as their enemy... Then, Arjuna, they too will gain me.

~ 12 ~

DEVOTION OR DISCIPLINE?

1

Arjuna: Some people always link personally to you through love, the supreme form of worship. Others link to your formless, unchanging aspect. Which of the two expresses a higher understanding of yoga?

2

Krishna: In my opinion, the higher understanding of yoga is expressed by those whose minds are enrapt in me, and always adore me with all their heart's conviction.

3-4

Arjuna: What about the others?

Krishna: Certainly they also achieve me. They scrupulously curtail their sensuality, develop absolute neutrality towards everyone and everything, and work only for the benefit of others. Thus they thoroughly worship my formless, undefined, unchanging, all-pervading, incomprehensible, innermost, and unwaveringly fixed aspect.

5

Arjuna: If they both attain you, why do you differentiate one as better than the other?

Krishna: Because it is very *difficult* to enwrap your mind in something undefined. It is only with great misery that an embodied soul can attain the goal by that abstract path.

6-7

Arjuna: Why is the path of devotion easier?

Krishna: Mostly because I personally reciprocate with the effort. My devotees dedicate all their efforts to me. Giving up everything else and making me their ultimate goal, they meditate upon me without deviation or distraction. How can I *not* personally respond?

When someone embraces me with their heart and mind I *personally* rescue them from the endless waves of death's ocean, very quickly.

8

Arjuna: How should I follow this path of devotion?

Krishna: Apply wisdom to your emotions and thoughts so that they remain always fixed upon me. Then, without a doubt, you will live in me forever.

9

Arjuna: What if my wisdom cannot always keep my thoughts and emotions on you?

Krishna: Arjuna, if your heart is not wise enough to naturally affix to me, then *practice* doing so. This will increase your natural desire for me.

10

Arjuna: What if I lack the discipline to fully apply myself to this practice?

Krishna: If you cannot practice fixing your heart and mind upon me, then fix your deeds upon me. If you work in my service you will advance towards perfection.

11

Arjuna: What if I cannot always dedicate myself to doing your deeds?

Krishna: Then do your own deeds, but give away all the rewards. This will make you more selfless and self-satisfied, improving your ability to follow the more direct paths of devotion I just mentioned.

12

Arjuna: OK, but what if I am unwilling to entirely give up the hard-earned fruits of my labor?

Krishna: Then you need to improve your philosophical understanding of things. When you have better knowledge, meditate upon it deeply. Then strive again to give away all the fruits of your labor, for doing so brings inner peace.[i]

13-14

Arjuna: What are the qualities of a person who progresses on the path you've outlined here?

Krishna: You will never feel hatred towards anyone. Instead you will always feel very friendly and compassionate. You will feel neither possessive nor

---

[i] Texts 8 through 12 convey message well worth reiterating:

8: The essence of *bhakti-yoga* is to enwrap your heart and mind in Krishna. The best way to do this is out of heartfelt desire to attain divine love, a desire that results from deep wisdom. *(rāgānugā-sādhana)*

9: When such heartfelt desires are absent, one should fall back upon the strength of willpower to keep one's heart and mind wrapped around Krishna. *(vaidhi-sādhana)*

10: If willpower is insufficient, one must at least engage in the physical actions of *bhakti-yoga*. *(karma-miśra bhakti-yoga)*

11: If we cannot do this, we fall outside the realm of *bhakti-yoga* but can still make progress towards it by giving away all the rewards of our actions. *(karma-yoga)*

12: If we can't do this, we need to get a deeper philosophy, contemplate it carefully, and keep trying.

important - being patient and looking upon pleasure and pain with an equal eye, always satisfied by your constant link to the divine. You will be self-disciplined and determined. Your emotions and thoughts will be enrapt in me. You will be in love with me, and I will be in love with you.

15

Arjuna: What qualities do you find most attractive?

Krishna: I am very attracted to anyone who never troubles others or feels troubled by them; unmotivated by the urges of thrills, desperations, and fears.

16-19

Arjuna: What do you find even more attractive?

Krishna: I am most attracted to my devotee - a very neutral, impartial, pure, and expertly balanced person who for my sake completely gives up all other aspirations and the disturbances they cause.

Anyone who completely gives up everything desirable and undesirable for the sake of divine love, never lamenting and hating an undesirable situation, and never hungering and yearning for a desirable one... oh, I find that person so attractive!

I am very attracted to anyone who, out of firm dedication to divine love, equally renounces the embrace of friends and enemies, honor and dishonor, hot and cold, pleasure and misery. They are equally silent in the face of insult or praise because they are fully self-satisfied in any situation. They do not even require a roof over their heads!

20

Arjuna: Of all these beautifully attractive qualities, which do you find the *most* irresistible?

Krishna: The most irresistibly attractive thing is when a person completely pours their heart and soul into the blissful and immortal principle that I am the highest object of love and devotion.

~ 13 ~

REAL KNOWLEDGE

1

Arjuna: I want to understand the world more clearly and philosophically. Then, I might develop the equipoise you are so attracted to. Please explain these three important pairs: *prakriti* and *puruṣa; kṣetra* and *kṣetra-jña;* and *jñāna* and *jñeya*.

2-3

Krishna: First I will explain *kṣetra* and *kṣetra-jña*.

Kṣetra means "field." The *field* refers to your field of activity: your body and the world it operates in.

Kṣetra-jña means "field-knower." The *field-knower* is *you*: consciousness, the soul in the body.

You are a conscious entity aware of a single field, but there is another "field-knower" who is a super-conscious entity aware of *all* fields. That is me.

This also relates to another term you asked about: *jñāna* - knowledge. It's my opinion that real "knowledge" is to clearly understand the field and the field-knowers.

4-5

Arjuna: Before going on to the topic of knowledge, please explain more about the field and the field-knowers.

Krishna: Listen carefully, I will summarize what many different sages, scriptures, and philosophical codes say about the field - how it works, and what it does - and about the field-knower's power.

6

Arjuna: Please go on.

Krishna: First I will explain the *field*. Your body, and the world it interacts with, is a mixture of various elements.

Arjuna: What are those elements?

Krishna: There are *five tangible elements*: solids, liquids, gasses, energies, and space.[i] Then there is *ego*, which makes one feel important enough to control and exploit these elements.

---

[i] A.k.a. "earth, water, air, fire, and ether" respectively.

Intellect is ego's immediate tool. And ego is the immediate tool of the *unseen background nature.*

Arjuna: Does intellect have a tool?

Krishna: It has the eleven senses. There are *five senses of input* (eyes, ears, nose, mouth, and skin) and *five senses of output* (voice, hands, legs, genital, and anus). These are controlled by the master sense: *the mind.*

Arjuna: Do the senses have tools?

Krishna: They have objects, *five sense-objects:* form, sound, scent, taste, and touch.

Arjuna: Is there anything else in the field?

Krishna: No. Everything in your body and world is a permutation of combinations of these 24 items.

7

Arjuna: What happens when these 24 parts combine and interact?

Krishna: Some combinations strike the mind as *attractive,* while others seem *repulsive.* This, in turn, generates emotions - which are all a variety of *happiness* or *distress.*[i]

Arjuna: So, emotions are in the field, not the field-knower?

---

[i] The mind judges one combination of elements to be "attractive" and another combination to be "repulsive." It experiences a sensation of "happiness" when it acquires what it finds attractive, or avoids what it finds repulsive. It experiences "distress" when it cannot acquire what it finds attractive, or cannot avoid what it finds repulsive.

Krishna: Yes, but the field-knower assembles a channel through which it witnesses these emotions and identifies with them.

Arjuna: What is that channel?

Krishna: Closest to the field-knower is the power of *will*, and then *sentience*, which links the field-knower to the specific arrangements of the 24 parts of the field, which form the *body* and world.

8

Arjuna: This is complex, what is the best way to gain a clear understanding of all this? Relating to my question about *jñāna* (knowledge), what is the true beginning of knowledge?

Krishna: The root of all knowledge is *humility* and *sincerity*. These make us *patient* and *honest*, essential qualities of good students who learn well.

Arjuna: What do good students learn from their teachers?

Krishna: First, *self-control*, which begins with *cleanliness* and *regularity*.

9

Arjuna: What is the essence of self-control?

Krishna: The essence of self-control is to diminish the ego and control its desire to exploit the sensual world.

Arjuna: How does the teacher help us do this?

Krishna: By helping us to be aware of the flaw inherent in our field.

Arjuna: What flaw?

Krishna: That birth leads to death, after dragging us through old age and illness.

10

Arjuna: What happens when ego starts to slacken its passion to exploit the sensual world?

Krishna: It is like being freed from an all-consuming addiction. It loosens our compulsive embrace on objects of pleasure like children, mates, and property. In that peaceful state, the mind feels ever-balanced, regardless of desired or undesired circumstances.

11

Arjuna: Is this peaceful state the final goal of knowledge, or is there something even more worthy beyond it?

Krishna: Peaceful detachment from the interactions of the field is the *beginning* of the greatest joy: true love. Once you are peaceful and non-exploitive you can then form an uninterrupted link of pure divine love with me, without any ulterior motive.

Desiring this link, you will lose all interest in common people and places, and instead seek a quiet, solitary residence.

12

Arjuna: Why seek solitude?

Krishna: You will want to be free from interruptions to contemplating your true self. You will not want to see anyone or anything except the object of true knowledge.

Arjuna: Is this quest for divine love the culmination of knowledge and education?

Krishna: True knowledge and education begins from humility and culminates in uninterrupted intimacy with the object of true knowledge. Anything outside what I have described is ignorance.

13

Arjuna: What is the *object of true knowledge*?

Krishna: The true object of knowledge *(jñeya)* is the beginningless spiritual energy that descends from me. The wise describe it as beyond both existence and non-existence. Those who know it experience immortal bliss.

14-18

Arjuna: How can I conceive of something that is beyond both existence and non-existence?

Krishna: Conceive of its hands, feet, eyes, heads, and faces everywhere. Know that it hears through every ear as it surrounds and permeates everything.

Know it as the power of illumination in all your senses, despite being far beyond all your senses. It has no affections, yet is very affectionate to everyone. It is beyond qualification, yet completely qualified.

It is within all living beings, yet beyond all of them. It is immovable, yet it moves. It is beyond full comprehension, because it is so subtle. It is very far away, but also very close.

It is indivisible, yet divided within everything. That object of knowledge creates, maintains, and destroys all things.

It is certainly the luminosity within all luminous things, so we describe it as "beyond darkness." It is knowledge, and the object of knowledge, and, within the hearts of all beings, it is approached through knowledge.

19

Arjuna's eyes were wide and unblinking. No words came from his awestruck mouth.

Krishna: I've answered your questions about the field, and explained that the field-knower is spirit. I explained that the supreme spirit is the ultimate object of knowledge; and I have described the process of attaining knowledge.

Arjuna: Yes... but who can fully understand what you have said?

Krishna: Someone like *you*. Those who have true devotion to me can comprehend all this in their effort to attain my intimate association.

20

Arjuna: That is encouraging. Now, please explain the remaining terms, *prakṛti* and *puruṣa*?

Krishna: What do you already know?

Arjuna: I know the dictionary meanings: *Prakṛti* means "energy," the thing from which other things are created. *Puruṣa* means "person," the conscious being. So, I surmise that *prakṛti* is matter, and *puruṣa* is spirit?

Krishna: Good. Go on.

Arjuna: So, since *prakṛti* is matter, it is synonymous with the "field-of-activity." As since *puruṣa* is spirit, it is synonymous with the "field-knower."

Krishna: Good, you understand. So what is your question?

Arjuna: How and when do the two become related?

Krishna: You must understand that matter *(prakṛti)* and spirit *(puruṣa)* are both eternal, beyond chronological origins. Their relationship has "no beginning."

Arjuna: How can matter be eternal? It is constantly being created and destroyed!

Krishna: Exactly. It is in an eternal state of change, endlessly cycling through various delimitations.

21

Arjuna: Spirit has no such changes?

Krishna: It doesn't change in the same way that matter does. It's understood that matter provides the mechanisms and substances of creation. Spirit experiences a *sensation* of change by identifying with these fluctuating substances. So it is understood that spirit's identification with matter provides the experience of emotional transformations, pleasures and pains.

22

Arjuna: How do matter and spirit become linked together?

Krishna: Spirit becomes enmeshed in matter because it wants to enjoy the various things available in the field. That is why spirit embraces qualification and delimitation, and takes birth in matter through various wombs.

23

Arjuna: Earlier, you mentioned that you are a type of field-knower, the knower of *all* fields. So, do you also become enmeshed in matter like this?

Krishna: No. I am a superior spiritual entity called *paramātmā* ("Super-soul"). I am the *true* controller, proprietor and enjoyer of the field.

Arjuna: What is its relationship between the Super-soul and the ordinary soul?

Krishna: The Supersoul oversees and authorizes the will of the ordinary soul.

24

Arjuna: What is the result of understanding all of this?

Krishna: Anyone who understands what I have said about spirit and the delimitations of matter will extricate their soul from material energy, and never again take birth within it.

25-26

Arjuna: How can I *really* understand all that you have explained?

Krishna: Some do it by meditation: focusing their inner self upon the self within themselves. Others do it by logic and reason. Still others do it by being responsibly dutiful. And then there are others who are not particularly qualified for any of these paths. They can also transcend mortal vision if they recourse to hearing about these topics from those who understand.

27-28

Arjuna: When they attain a realized vision of the world, what do they see?

Krishna: "Everything that will ever exist anywhere, sentient or inert, arises from the combination of the field and field-knower." They *see* this.

The Supreme Master is equally situated in all entities. Things that appear to be destroyed are indestructible. They see this because they truly see.

29

Arjuna: What results from such vision?

Krishna: If you see God equally situated everywhere your mind will never lose touch with your soul. Therefore you will achieve the supreme goal.

30

Arjuna: There are so many different people and things - how is it possible to see oneness and equality?

Krishna: These differences are in the field only, not in the field-knower. All deeds and endeavors occur in, and by, the field. The field-knower is not truly involved in any of it. That is real vision, try to see it.

31

Arjuna: So, to see oneness I have to focus on seeing the soul in everyone and everything?

Krishna: Yes, but even if you focus only upon the field, you will find it is all essentially one, despite the infinite variations in its appearance. All the very different external manifestations of things are simply expansions from the singularity of the field. Try to *see* the truth of this theory and you will have a spiritual vision of the world.

32

Arjuna: Does the field-knower blend into the field and become something new, something different from what it originally was?

Krishna: Not really. Arjuna, the field-knower dwells within the body but does *not* blend into it and does not truly do anything with it. The field-knower is a causeless entity, beyond delimitations, inexhaustible, and superior to the field.

33

Arjuna: How can the soul be within the body, yet not blend into and become implicated in it?

Krishna: Isn't space within everything yet quite distinct from everything as well? Similarly, the soul is spread all throughout the body, yet remains distinct and unblended.

34-35

Arjuna: If it does not blend with the body, what is the point of spreading through it?

Krishna: To spread the illumination of consciousness! The Sun is another example of something that spreads everywhere yet remains distinct. Just as one sun illuminates the entire world, the field-knower illuminates the entire body with consciousness.

Those who see the body and soul with the inner eye of knowledge liberate their spirit from matter and progress towards the Supreme.

~ 14 ~

THREE QUALITIES
OF THE FIELD

1

Arjuna: Would you elaborate on what you've just explained, especially about the field of activities?

Krishna: Yes, I will continue to explain the best of all sciences. The sages who understood this science attained the supreme perfections.

2

Arjuna: What "supreme perfections"?

Krishna: They attained a condition similar to mine.

Arjuna: "Similar" in what way?

Krishna: They attained a state of being that is beyond the universe: not activated by creation or terminated by destruction.

3

Arjuna: I am eager to learn this science and attain similar achievements! Please begin to explain the field in more detail.

Krishna: The world originates from a singularity we can call *mahad-brahma* - "The Great Self-Existent." It is something like my womb, which I impregnate to give birth to everything in the universe.

4

Arjuna: Then you are the mother and father of everything?

Krishna: Essentially.

Arjuna: I have a mother and father, though. I wasn't born from you.

Krishna: My dear cousin, my singularity is the womb of all other wombs. And I am the *original* seed-giving father.

5

Arjuna: Creations spring from other creations?

Krishna: Right.

Arjuna: What is the *first* creation of the singularity?

Krishna: The first child of the singularity is "Nature" (*prakṛti*). Nature is an entity with three qualities: *sattva*, *rajas*, and *tamas*. These are the three ropes that bind a limitless being into a limited body, my strong friend.

6-9

Arjuna: Can you explain more about each quality?

Krishna: *Sattva* is clear and undistorted and therefore allows the illumination of consciousness to shine brightly. It binds with the rope of preference for happiness and comprehension.

Rajas is distorted and dimmed by passion. It binds the living being in ropes of ever-rising thirsts and efforts.

Tamas is the strongest of all. It eclipses with ignorance and thus bewilders every soul. It has many ropes, like negligence, laziness and stagnation.

In summary: *Sattva* creates happiness. *Rajas* creates effort. *Tamas* eclipses knowledge and creates negligence.

10

Arjuna: How do these three qualities produce all the varieties we see in nature?

Krishna: Every aspect of the field results from a unique combination of all three qualities. In some objects, *sattva* is more prominent than the others. In some, *rajas* is most prominent. In others, *tamas* is the most prominent quality.

11-13

Arjuna: How can I tell which quality is prominent?

Krishna: When *sattva* is prominent, all the "doors" of the body are bright and clear, producing knowledge and understanding.

When *rajas* is prominent, it generates lust, restlessness, new efforts, and greedy accumulation.

When *tamas* is prominent, is creates darkness, laziness, negligence, and illusion.

14-15

Arjuna: What is the ultimate result of the influence of each quality?

Krishna: If you accumulate *sattva*, after death you will go to the pure regions of the very wise. If you have attained *rajas* you will be reborn among those who embrace passionate work. If you die in *tamas* you are reborn from the wombs of fools.

16

Arjuna: What is the *immediate* result of each quality?

Krishna: *Sattva* produces a pure result because it inspires deeds that are very pure. However, *rajas* results in unhappiness and *tamas* results in ignorance.

17-18

Arjuna: How do these results come about?

Krishna: The three qualities come to their immediate and final ends as a result of their primary effects: *sattva* gives rise to knowledge, *rajas* to strong greeds, and *tamas* to negligence, illusion, and ignorance. That is why *sattva* leads to the highest results, *rajas* to ordinary results, and *tamas* leads down to vile results.

19-20

Arjuna: You said that sages attain an existence like your own by understanding all this. How is that possible?

Krishna: If you can perceive the three qualities of nature you will be able to see for yourself that all your deeds are little more than the interactions of these three qualities, and that you are distinct from and superior to all of them. This understanding will carry you to an existence like my own.

When you surpass the three qualities that bind you to a limited bodily existence, you will become completely free from birth, death, old age, and sadness; and you will delight in immortal nectar.

21

Arjuna: My competent friend, what are the essential qualities of people who have surpassed the three qualities? What is their behavior? How do they rise beyond these qualities?

22-23

Krishna: If you rise beyond the three qualifiers of nature: You will not love or hate the flourishing or abatement of any of the symptoms of the three qualities, like illumination, accumulation, or illusion. You will be seated neutrally, apart from such things, unmoved by them, knowing, "This is just the business of nature's qualities." Thus you will be very firm and never waver.

24-25

Arjuna: How would this reflect in my behavior?

Krishna: When you do not invest yourself into these qualities you will remain situated within your true self. You will therefore feel equal towards every pleasure and displeasure. You will treat gold as you treat any stone or dirt. You will treat the unwanted as you treat the dear. You will treat criticism and dishonor as you treat great honor and praise. You will treat enemies as you treat friends. You will completely give up all new enterprises and efforts, considering all results to be the same. Then you would be known as one who is beyond the qualities of nature.

26

Arjuna: How can I rise beyond the three qualities and attain this exalted condition?

Krishna: If you unwaveringly serve me with affection you will thoroughly surpass these qualities and become a spiritual being.

27

Arjuna: Why is it that by loving you one becomes spiritual?

Krishna: Because I am the foundation of spirituality - the essence of the inexhaustible fountain of immortal, ceaseless, penultimate pleasure.

~ 15 ~

BEYOND THE UNIVERSE

1-4

Arjuna: You talked about going beyond the three qualities of this universe. Can you describe what lies beyond the universe?

Krishna: They say this world is a phantasmal Banyan tree, upside-down, with roots going up and branches going down. Promises of enjoyment flutter in the breeze as its leaves. To realize those promises, you must know the tree very well.

Watered by the three qualities of nature, its branches expand in all directions, upwards and downwards, and finally produce buds of enjoyable sense objects. From these branches, roots also fall downwards and find nourishment in the selfish deeds of the mortal world.

The real tree is elsewhere. This is merely a reflection, with no end, no beginning, and no real substance. No one can uproot this tree, but you must tenaciously cut it down with the axe of indifference to it.

Once it is felled, seek out what is beyond it: a place from which no one ever strays. Once there, seek the Original Person – the ancient one from whom the true tree grows – and give yourself wholly to him.

5

Arjuna: How can I possibly succeed in such an amazing quest?

Krishna: Be free from the intoxication of honor and cast off your faulty entourage. Dwell always in yourself, and curb down external lusts. Free yourself from dualities like pleasure and displeasure. Then you can successfully attain that foolproof, eternal destination.

6

Arjuna: What is this destination like?

Krishna: The sun does not shine there, nor the moon, nor fire. In that place from which no one strays, *I* am the supreme illumination.

7-8

Arjuna: What creatures dwell in the upside-down tree?

Krishna: The living creatures in this living world are certainly eternal fragments of me. Situating themselves within material nature, they draw unto themselves six sensual capacities, headed by the mind.

Thus the soul develops and dissolves its bodies. Like the wind carrying a scent, the soul carries the subtle elements of one body into the next.

9-11

Arjuna: Why does the soul change bodies?

Krishna: Different bodies offer different arrays of sense perception. The soul changes bodies because it wishes to enjoy sense objects in various ways.

The soul stays in a body for some time and then gives it up after enjoying its wealth and qualities. Those with informed vision can see this, but great fools cannot recognize it, even when shown.

Serious spiritualists see the soul doing all these things, but those who are serious to avoid the soul are basically unconscious, and thus blind to it.

12-14

Arjuna: How can those without well-developed spiritual vision eventually come to perceive spiritual things?

Krishna: By making an effort to perceive me in whatever they *can* already see.

Arjuna: Please give some examples.

Krishna: The brilliance of the sun, illuminating the whole entire world, and the brilliance of the moon and fire - it is *my* brilliance. I am in the Earth, empowering her to support all creatures with her produce. I am in the Moon, empowering vegetation to be delicious and nourishing. I am in the bodies of all breathing creatures as the fire which mixes with breath and allows you to digest the different foods you prepare from your harvests.

15

Arjuna: So, by carefully and wisely observing this world - as is done in empirical sciences - one can gain knowledge and become aware of you?

Krishna: Yes. I am certainly the true object of knowledge in all science. I created the sciences, and only I truly comprehend them. Yet, I share this knowledge. From within everyone's heart, I allow people to comprehend or ignore it.

16-20

Arjuna: Then it seems you are very intimately connected to every soul. Please explain a bit about your position in comparison to the soul.

Krishna: In this world, people have two aspects: one transient and one perpetual. All creatures are transient in appearance, while their inner being is perpetual. Yet there is another, *ultimate* being: "Supersoul." He is the inexhaustible master who enters the three worlds to sustain them. I am that Supersoul.

I am certainly beyond transience, and beyond permanence, too. Therefore I am called "ultimate." That is why the wise celebrate me as "The Ultimate Person."

Anyone who understands me clearly understands everything. Arjuna my dear friend, that person comes to adore me in all ways.

I have just explained the deepest secrets of the scriptures. Comprehend what I have said, and you shall become extremely intelligent, and your deeds will be flawless.

~ 16 ~

CLIMBING AND DESCENDING THE TREE

1-4

Arjuna: What are the fruits on the tree that is the world?

Krishna: There are two types of fruits: one that elevates and another that degrades.

Arjuna: Which fruits elevate the person who eats them?

Krishna: These "fruits" are godly character-traits: fearlessness, purity, generosity, self-discipline, sacrifice, simplicity, steadiness, study, being guided by spiritual wisdom, nonviolence, honesty, non-anger, renunciation, peacefulness, non-criticism, compassion for all creatures, desirelessness, gentility, modesty, reliability, empowerment, forgiveness, forbearance, cleanliness, non-enviousness, and non-arrogance.

Arjuna: Which fruits degrade the person who eats them?

Krishna: All the ungodly traits, especially ignorance, and pretension, vanity, arrogance, anger, and insolence.

5

Arjuna: Unfortunately, I recognize those traits in myself.

Krishna: That is because you are humble, and thus godly, my friend.

Arjuna: Where does "elevation" lead?

Krishna: Eventually, to liberation.

Arjuna: And "degradation," where does that lead?

Krishna: It only tightens your shackles.

Arjuna: What types of people eat these two types of fruits?

Krishna: The godly eat the auspicious fruits of the tree, and thus elevate towards liberation. The ungodly eat the inauspicious fruits and thus descend deeper into bondage.

6-16

Arjuna: How does one recognize an ungodly personality?

Krishna: The ungodly cannot distinguish loss from gain. They don't understand honesty, morality, or purity.

Arjuna: What philosophy do they live by?

Krishna: They believe that the world is unreal, without substance and without a master. They say it results by chance and therefore has no purpose except to be exploited by their lust.

With this ignorant outlook, they destroy themselves and promote ugly ways of life that ruin and torment the world.

Completely dedicated to insatiable lust, they intoxicate themselves on the madness of pretentious prestige. In the grips of delusion they make impure plans to grasp for unreal things.

They believe that sense gratification is the ultimate goal of life, so their endless worries endure until the day they die. The flames of lust and anger constantly consume them, but they cannot escape because they are bound in the ropes of hundreds of desires.

Driven by selfishness and intoxicated by ignorance, they amass dirty money, thinking, "So far I have made so much profit, but still I want much more! I want this, and that… and soon I will have the wealth to get it all! I have already done away with my opponents, and I will certainly destroy anyone else who gets in my way. I am the master! I am the enjoyer! I am accomplished, powerful, and happy. Is there anyone else in the world as opulent as I, surrounded as I am by aristocracy and celebrity? I will celebrate my glory by holding sacrifices and giving gifts!"

Bewildered by countless ambitions, caught in the nets of delusion, and addicted to sense gratification, they fall into a filthy, hellish world.

17-20

Arjuna: You said they perform sacrifice and give gifts. Those arc good deeds! Why then should they fall into hell?

Krishna: Their hypocritical religion and morality is merely lip-service, employed to further inflate their false prestige. It is not true sacrifice or charity. They are too stubborn and full of themselves, enthralled by their own power and money.

The truth is that they are envious and hateful of me, who am within their own body and in everyone else's, too. They have surrendered themselves instead to ego, power, vanity, lust, and anger. Therefore they get no benefit from their ostentatious piety.

Those cruel and hateful subhumans *belong* in this material world, so I repeatedly put them into the unfortunate wombs of the darkened. Spending birth after birth amongst these darkened and bewildered people, they migrate towards the lowest destinies, never seeking me.

21-22

Arjuna: How can they escape from this situation?

Krishna: There are three dark gates in and out of this hellish self-destruction: lust, anger, and greed. If anyone gives up these three qualities, the gates release them and they can then do themselves the greatest good by proceeding towards the topmost destination.

23-24

Arjuna: How can anyone give up these three dark qualities?

Krishna: The rules of scriptural authority exist for that purpose. If someone casts aside such rules they will remain at the whims of their lusts, and it will be impossible to accomplish anything, experience happiness, or attain the topmost destination. Therefore humanity should avail herself of this authority to clearly determine the dos and don'ts of daily affairs. This will regulate their lust and grant them escape from degradation.[i]

---

[i] The vast majority of religious scripture is sociological. It gives rules and regulations regarding how to pursue selfish desires in a "moral" manner. Although this is hardly the purest form of spirituality, it is very useful because it affords selfish people a way to begin regulating, controlling and moderating their desires. This causes a gradual evolution that eventually enables them to participate in much more noble and pure forms of spirituality.

~ 17 ~

TYPES OF FAITH

1

Arjuna: You said that following scriptural authority is important. What about people who lead good lives with great faith, but ignore the specific dos and don'ts of scriptural authority?

2-3

Krishna: Please listen carefully. Faith not only makes you who you are, it is also an expression of who you are. So when it does not come from scriptures it comes instead from our natural character. Since there are three basic types of character, there are three basic types of such faith: *sattva* (clear), *rajas* (passionate), and *tamas* (dark).

4

Arjuna: How can I distinguish the three types of faith?

Krishna: One way is by the object of that faith. If the object of faith is divine, that faith is divine: *sattva*. If the object is a passionate natural force, that faith is passionate: *rajas*. If the object is a dark ghostly entity, that faith is dark: *tamas*.

5-6

Arjuna: Some people do not have a specific object of worship. They simply perform austerities. What type of faith is this?

Krishna: Those who subject themselves to ghastly austerities not recommended by scriptural authorities are almost always totally obsessed with ambitions and lusts, saturated by conceit and self-importance. They mindlessly torture the elements of their body, their soul, and even me, the Supersoul who also dwells in their bodies. Understand that these people have *demonic* faith.

7

Arjuna: I understand. Please continue explaining how to differentiate the three types of faith.

Krishna: Everyone prefers different types of food, ceremonies, austerities, and charities. I will explain how to differentiate faith on the basis of such preferences.

8-10

Arjuna: What types of diet symptomize the three types of faith?

Krishna: A person with clear faith *(sattva)* is fond of food that is juicy, mild, and substantial, which grants long life, calmness, strength, health, happiness and satisfaction.

A person with passionate faith *(rajas)* wants food that is exaggerated: very bitter, sour, salty, spicy, pungent, or astringent. These foods cause unhappiness and regret, because they invite illness.

A person with dark faith *(tamas)* likes to eat things that are old, dry, smelly, stale, left-over, and disgusting.

11-13

Arjuna: How do ceremonies symptomize the three types of faith?

Krishna: A person with clear faith *(sattva)* performs ceremonies as a matter of duty, not to fulfill some personal ambition.

A person with passionate faith *(rajas)* performs ceremonies because they desire some result, especially to inflate their status.

A person with dark faith *(tamas)* performs ceremonies without believing in them, and therefore makes no effort to follow rules, feed people at the ceremony, chant the mantras, or give charity.

14-16

Arjuna: What about austerity? Previously you described austerity as a symptom of demonic faith.

Krishna: Uncontrolled and wild austerity is demoniac, but austerity can also be a valid aspect of religion. Let me explain more clearly what "austerity" really is: It is, essentially, any *effort* made by the body, words, or mind.

Arjuna: What are the recommended austerities in each category?

Krishna: Bodily austerity is the effort to always give deference to others - particularly to gods, priests, teachers, and the wise. It is also the effort to be clean, simple, celibate, and non-violent.

Verbal austerity is the effort to speak the truth in a manner that is affectionate, helpful, and not unsettling. It is also the discipline of voicing the recitations that are part of your studies.

Mental austerity is the effort towards self-control through emotional contentment, gentleness, silence, and improvement of one's character.

17-19

Arjuna: How do the three types of faith implement these austerities?

Krishna: A person with clear faith *(sattva)* steadily performs these three types of austerities without selfish motive.

A person with passionate faith *(rajas)* does austerity proudly, to become more important, honored, and respected. They do not practice very diligently or steadfastly.

A person with dark faith *(tamas)* does austerity foolishly, out of self-loathing or with a hope to destroy others.

20-22

Arjuna: What types of charity epitomize the three types of faith?

Krishna: A person with clear faith *(sattva)* gives charity because it is the right thing to do, not because they will get something in return. They give charity in proper situations, at appropriate times, to deserving persons.

A person with passionate faith *(rajas)* gives charity for the sake of gaining something in return. They do not really want to give, but they feel they must.

A person with dark faith *(tamas)* gives in the wrong situations, at inappropriate times, to undeserving persons, disrespectfully and carelessly.

23-28

Arjuna: How do I improve the quality of my faith?

Krishna: Always remember the phrase, *"oṁ tat sat."* These three words describe the supreme spirit. Since ancient times, these words have directed our attention to the spiritual essence within rituals and ceremonies. That is why it is a rule that the word *"oṁ"* must prefix a spiritualist's every ceremony, charity, austerity, and deed.

The word *"tat"* reminds us that our ceremonies, charities, austerities and deeds should be done for *"oṁ"* - for spiritual aims such as liberation, not for petty material rewards.

The word *"sat"* indicates reality and goodness. Good deeds therefore begin with the sound of *"sat."* It reminds us that reality is within our ceremonies, austerities, charities, and deeds, and that these things should all be done only for the sake of reality and goodness.

Any sacrifice, gift, effort. or deed undertaken without this conviction is unreal and amounts to nothing, neither in this life nor after death.

~ 18 ~

CONCLUSION OF WISDOM

1

Arjuna: You are powerful and can destroy all obstacles, so please answer a few questions to clarify everything you have explained.

Krishna: Of course, go ahead and ask.

Arjuna: What is the difference between internal and external renunciation?

2

Krishna: External renunciation affects your external behavior: you give up all actions that attempt to satisfy your personal desires. Internal renunciation affects your internal motivations: you give up the desire to enjoy the rewards of your deeds.

3

Arjuna: Which is better?

Krishna: There are different opinions among the wise. Some say that actions are inherently selfish and therefore should be given up entirely. Others say that actions like sacrifice, charity and austerity shouldn't be given up.

4-6

Arjuna: What is your opinion? Tell me that and I will be confident.

Krishna: I firmly agree that actions like sacrifice, charity, and austerity should never be abandoned; for they purify even the wise. But still, my friend, such actions must be performed with a high grade of internal renunciation - as a matter of duty, not as a tool for selfish aims.

Arjuna: What is "high grade"?

Krishna: There are three grades of renunciation.

7-10

Arjuna: What are they?

Krishna: Those in darkness *(tamas)* are confused, and therefore give up responsibilities that should never be forsaken.

Passionate people *(rajas)* want pleasure, and therefore give up any responsibility that seems difficult and disturbing. This will never grant the fruit of true renunciation.

Those in clarity *(sattva)* never give up, they carry out their responsibilities thinking, "This is my duty." What they renounce is any claim to the rewards of those actions. They don't detest unpleasant work, nor are they particularly attached to pleasant deeds. These intelligent people are free of all doubts and completely clear about renunciation.

11

Arjuna: Renunciation in clarity, which is best, seems identical to internal renunciation. So, it seems you are saying that internal renunciation is better than external renunciation?

Krishna: Yes, because it is impossible for any living being to renounce *all* activities. Being a "renunciate" really means giving up the rewards of all your actions.

12

Arjuna: Since it is *internal* it is difficult to observe or measure. How can I measure my degree of internal renunciation?

Krishna: The more you worry about the outcomes of your deeds - desirable, undesirable, or mixed - the less is your internal renunciation. When your internal renunciation is perfect, you have no such worries at all.

13-17

Arjuna: Even if I gave up all interest in the rewards of my actions, I would still perform actions. Since every action has a reaction, how could I possibly become free while still engaged in action?

Krishna: When you give up your personal interest in an activity you will realize that you are not the true performer of that deed. Thus you will no longer be the true recipient of its reaction.

Arjuna: How is it possible that I am not the true agent of my own actions?

Krishna: My friend, our science describes *five* agents in any action.

Arjuna: What are they?

Krishna: They are the venue, performer, instruments, techniques, and, of course, divinity.

The venue is the world your body inhabits; the performer is your ego. The instruments are your senses; the techniques are the movements of muscles and so forth that utilize those senses. And divinity is the Supersoul. These five are the true causes of every action you perform with your body, words, or even your thoughts.

As long as you see yourself as the sole agent of your deeds, you have not yet developed real intelligence, and stupidity will blind you. Don't let your intellect be shackled and bound by such an egoistic concepts. Realize that you are not the true agent of your action and even if destiny forces you to kill all these soldiers you will never be bound to the worldly reactions of such deeds.

18

Arjuna: It seems that intelligence and knowledge is the key to being freed from karma?

Krishna: Yes. Knowledge and action are inseparably linked. You always act based on what you understand. Thus, knowledge is the foundation and inspiration of action.

Arjuna: Can you describe knowledge and action more clearly?

Krishna: Knowledge has three aspects: the thing that knows, the thing that is known, and the faculty of knowing. Action has three similar aspects: The person who acts, the action itself, and the means by which it is accomplished.

19

Arjuna: Are knowledge and action affected by the three qualities of nature?

Krishna: Of course. Listen carefully and I will explain three types of knowledge, three types of action, and three types of actors - with reference to the three qualities: clarity *(sattva)*, passion *(rajas)*, and darkness *(tamas)*.

20-22

Arjuna: What are the three types of knowledge?

Krishna: Clear knowledge perceives the oneness and infinite eternality of all beings. It sees unity within the differences.

Passionate knowledge, however, sees only the temporary divisions and differences between all beings.

Darkened knowledge is very meager. Limited to tangible practicalities, it doesn't care much to comprehend causes or essences.

23-25

Arjuna: What are the three types of action?

Krishna: Clear action is not motivated by rewards. It is done as a duty, unconcerned with affinity or aversion to the deed.

Passionate action is motivated by the lust to enjoy its reward, or the sense of power and importance it conveys. These deeds are very exhausting.

Darkened action begins in a stupor, is executed without care, and winds up in pain, destruction, and debilitation.

Arjuna: I think I see the link between action and knowledge. *Clear* knowledge sees the oneness in all things, so when it acts it does not covet a particular reward or judge some things desirable and others undesirable. *Passionate* knowledge sees things as being intrinsically different, and thus strongly differentiates between desirable and undesirable deeds and rewards. *Darkened* knowledge is careless, and so are the actions it leads to. Is that right?

Krishna: Excellent!

26-28

Arjuna: Please describe the three types of actors.

Krishna: The clear actor has no selfishness, and thus no attachment to the rewards of action. Therefore her enthusiasm and determination never fluctuates in the face of success or failure.

The passionate actor is very attached to gaining the rewards of his actions. So, he is greedy and prone to harm people and be impure if necessary. He rejoices abundantly on success, and laments terribly on failure.

The darkened actor is base and materialistic. She is unqualified to succeed, but too stubborn to improve. Instead she resorts to lying and criticizing others. Lazy and procrastinate, she is always miserable in failure.

29

Arjuna: This information is so useful!

Krishna: Then I will tell you more, my friend, on related topics. I will describe the three types of intellect and willpower possessed by the three actors.

30-32

Arjuna: Yes, please explain the three types of intellect.

Krishna: Clear intellect accurately differentiates things: bondage from freedom, gain from loss, what should and shouldn't be done, what should and shouldn't be feared...

Passionate intellect cannot differentiate those things clearly.

Darkened intellect differentiates things incorrectly, mistaking immorality for morality, and always getting things backwards.

33-35

Arjuna: What are the three types of willpower?

Krishna: Clear willpower has a firm control over of the mind, life, senses, and deeds - engaging them in uninterrupted divine union.

Passionate willpower latches on to materialistic results, motivated by attachment and desire for specific rewards.

Darkened willpower is foolish and cannot break free from dreams, fears, lamentation, melancholy, and delusion.

36-39

Arjuna: What happiness do these three types of people enjoy?

Krishna: Happiness is the onset of pleasure and the cessation of suffering. There are three types:

The happiness of clarity tastes like poison in the beginning but ends up just like nectar. It comes as a gift of self-comprehension.

The happiness of passion tastes like nectar in the beginning but ends up like poison. It comes from sensual contact.

The happiness of darkness is only self-delusion in the beginning *and* at the end. It comes from sleep, laziness, and intoxication.

Arjuna: I think I understand how all these are connected.

Krishna: Then, please summarize what I explained about clarity.

Arjuna: Clarity sees the unity in all things. Clear people don't differentiate "desirable" from "undesirable." Thus their actions are motivated not by desire but by duty. Their intellect is set on clarifying what is their duty and what is not. Their willpower is fixed on not allowing themselves to be deviated from their duty. Although this all seems to disciplined and strict, clear people are the happiest of all because by stilling their external self they come into contact with their blissful inner self.

Krishna: Very good. What about passion?

Arjuna: Passion sees things as being essentially different. Therefore passionate people find some things "desirable" and others "undesirable." Based on that, they act with the motive to obtain the desirable and avoid the undesirable; they don't act out of duty. Their intellect doesn't care to distinguish what is dutiful from what is not; it is obsessed instead with differentiating the desirable from the undesirable. They apply their willpower to achieve the things they desire. Although this seems like fun, it winds up exhausting and lands them in conflict and misery.

Krishna: Excellent, and darkness?

Arjuna: Darkness doesn't really care about anything, so it produces haphazard and aimless actions. The darkened criticize others but do nothing themselves, except procrastinate. Their intellect doesn't distinguish between anything - everything is the same to them: duty and non-duty, desirable and undesirable. Therefore they have no ambition or willpower for anything other than fantasy and dreams. Happiness never really exists for them, outside of dreams.

Krishna: Very good!

40

Arjuna: Does *everyone* fall into one of these three categories?

Krishna: On earth and even among the gods in heaven, no being is free from the habitual nature that arises from the combination of these three forces.

41

Arjuna: Can you explain the categories of humans living on earth?

Krishna: My friend, we can categorize humanity into four groups as a result of the deeds they do, impelled by the personality generated in them by these three forces.

Arjuna: What are those four categories?

Krishna: The basic *(śūdra)*, the resourceful *(vaiśya)*, the protectors *(kṣatriya)*, and the intellectuals *(brahmaṇa)*.

42

Arjuna: What deeds place one in the intellectual category?

Krishna: Intellectuals must be impartial, self-controlled, spartan, clean, patient, honest, knowledgeable, wise, and fixed on the divine.

43

Arjuna: What about the protectors?

Krishna: Protectors must be heroic, powerful, steadfast, and expert. They must never flee from battle, be generous, and have the ability and inclination to control and direct others.

44

Arjuna: The resourceful?

Krishna: They must generate resources by farming, tending cows, and doing commerce.

Arjuna: The basic?

Krishna: They must do whatever is required of them by the other three.

45

Arjuna: What is the point of categorizing people in these four groups?

Krishna: Each person can gain great perfections by following the deeds prescribes as duties for their personality type.

46

Arjuna: Please explain more about this.

Krishna: Please listen carefully. Any type of person can attain perfection simply by doing their own natural deeds in the spirit of worshipping the divine - he from whom all things come, and who is within all things.

47-49

Arjuna: I am a warrior, a "protector." So it is my duty not to flee from this battle. But the duties of an intellectual seem more "spiritual" and pristine than mine. Wouldn't it be good for me to give up being a warrior and become an intellectual?

Krishna: Your own duty may seem ugly at times, and the duties of others may seem so attractive. But your own duty always leads to the best long-term result. Performing your own duty never truly leads to any misfortune.

Every deed has some imperfection, some flaw. "Even fire is marred by smoke." So don't be attached or averse to anything. Conquer your instincts and cast out their desires. Then you truly attain the perfection of "freedom from deeds" and become the best type of "renunciate."

50

Arjuna: What good will that serve?

Krishna: You will surpass all imperfection and gain perfection; you will achieve a spiritual existence.

Arjuna: How will the ghastly duties of a warrior grant me a "spiritual existence"?

Krishna: The act of self-control in abiding by your duty will generate realized, tangible knowledge - which carries you into transcendence.

51-53

Arjuna: If I was already situated in such knowledge, what would be my duty?

Krishna: You would then use your very pure intellect to firmly regulate your mental and emotional being. You would give up the sights and sounds of all things. You would set aside all dualities of love and hate.

Then, you would take fully to a life of renunciation: living in an isolated place; eating very lightly; and restraining your words, deeds, and thoughts in the constant endeavor to attain meditation.

You would practice selflessness and placidity by purifying yourself from self-importance, power, arrogance, lust, anger, and accumulation. Then you would tangibly become a spiritual being.

54

Arjuna: If I were a completely spiritual being, what would be my duty?

Krishna: In true tranquility, free from hungers and miseries, seeing the sameness of everyone and everything, you would then pursue the duty to set your heart fully upon my love.

55

Arjuna: If I were to succeed and attain pure love for you, what then?

Krishna: Through love it becomes possible to directly perceive me, as a tangible reality.

Arjuna: What happens when I directly perceive your reality?

Krishna: Then you would *enter* that reality, forevermore.

56

Arjuna: My dear friend, I see you, I love you, and I am in your reality - yet I am not peaceful. I am beset with this perplexing and disturbing war.

Krishna: There are always so many challenges. Face them all. Do all your duties completely relying on me. By my grace you will indeed attain the eternal, flawless position.

57

Arjuna: Please explain how to completely rely on you.

Krishna: In all cases, use your heart to understand if you should give up an action or if you can perform it for my sake. This yoga of intelligence will shelter you, and your heart will constantly be enrapt in me.

58

Arjuna: What happens then?

Krishna: When your heart is enrapt in me, you will rise above all the most difficult obstacles, by my grace. If self-centeredness prevents you from heeding these words, destruction will claim you.

59

Arjuna: How so?

Krishna: If you take shelter of self-centeredness, you will conclude, "I shall not fight." But this is all ridiculous; your fundamental character is to be a warrior, and you cannot so easily escape that!

60

Arjuna: How can you be so sure?

Krishna: My friend, people are *bound* to the deeds that express their fundamental character. It is a dream to think you can go against it. You will certainly be forced to follow your habits.

61-62

Arjuna: No one can deny what you are saying. But, I am habituated to self-centeredness. It forms an infinite loop I cannot escape. I feel like I am strapped helplessly on a machine made of selfish habits!

Krishna: Arjuna, everyone moves like robots under the spell of habits. But do not forget that the Master is at the heart of both the self and the machine! *Seek his shelter in all respects*, my dear friend. By his grace you will find and come into an eternal place of supreme peace.

63

Arjuna is silent.

Krishna: Now I have explained to you secret knowledge, and knowledge that is beyond secret. Consider it carefully and fully; and then, my friend, do as you will.

64-65

Arjuna is grave, silent, and serious for a long time.

Like the moon sprinkling cool light upon a gentle, white lotus, Krishna's butter-soft heart melts as he glances lovingly upon Arjuna with wide, gentle eyes set beneath exquisite eyebrows on a moon-like face framed in soft, black curls.

Krishna: My love, you are so very dear to me. Let me say something else to help you. Please hear my supreme instruction - the secret beyond all secrets:

Become my devotee by always thinking of me, worshipping me, or bowing to me. Then you will certainly come to me. This is the truth. I promise you. I love you and could never lie to you.

66

Arjuna: My dear Krishna, do I have any other duty?

Krishna: No, none! Abandon them all and run to me, and me alone!

Arjuna: If giving myself to you requires me to pain others…

Krishna: I am your shelter! I will personally take care of everything, and liberate you from all other responsibilities. Don't worry at all!

67-71

Arjuna is silent.

Krishna: There is nothing beyond this to explain.

If you ever want to share our conversation with others, don't waste time with the self-indulgent who are inherently averse to divine love. Do not speak of these things to anyone who will not carefully listen. And certainly do not bother with those who hate me.

But whoever explains these supreme secrets to those who *are* inclined towards my love, I will doubtlessly take into my personal company as my transcendental lover! No one would ever become more dear to me.

I feel that whoever reads and learns our sacred conversation has worshipped me through knowledge! Even if one only casually listens, yet does so without hatred and with just a little confidence in what they hear, they will be freed from misfortune and attain the blessed realms attained by the pious.

72

Arjuna: I will always remember this conversation and explain it to others who deserve to hear.

Krishna: Thank you, my friend. But, let's concern ourselves with you first. Have you listened to my explanations with a focused mind? Has your confusion been destroyed?

73

Arjuna: My dear, infallible friend, your compassion has destroyed my confusion and granted me wisdom. I am ready to carry out your instructions with confidence, free of doubt.

74-78

My dear reader, you have read my best understanding of the conversation between two great souls: Krishna and Arjuna. The amazing things I've shared with you set my hairs on end and bring tears to my eyes.

The grace of Śrī Guru has allowed me to somewhat comprehend and communicate this divine conversation to you. I never tire of this tale. With each telling it becomes more amazing, more deeply delightful - inspiring my vision of the wondrous, infinitely enchanting, extremely heart-stealing beauty of Krishna as he speaks to Arjuna.

> *Where there is the master of mysticism, Krishna*
> *Where there is the archer, Arjuna*
> *There is beauty, victory, and glory*
> *Unwavering and right.*
> *This is my opinion.*